WORLD PAYCHECKS

WHO MAKES WHAT, WHERE, AND WHY

WORLD PAYCHECKS

WHO MAKES WHAT, WHERE, AND WHY

by

DAVID HARROP

FACTS ON FILE, Inc.
460 Park Avenue South
New York, N.Y. 10016

WORLD PAYCHECKS

Published by Facts On File,Inc., 460 Park Avenue South, New York, N.Y. 10016

Library of Congress Cataloging in Publication Data

Harrop, David.
  World paychecks.

  Includes index.
  1. Wages. I. Title.
HD4906.H28   331.2'2   82-1463
ISBN 0-87196-531-3   AACR2

Printed and bound in the United States of America

9   8   7   6   5   4   3   2   1

CONTENTS

INTRODUCTION

Civilization is the accumulated result of the work done by billions of people since long before history began to chronicle their toil. The vast majority of these workers—certainly in the past and even in the present—have seen only the drudgery of their own tasks and have been but vaguely aware, if at all, of how their particular efforts fit into a larger scheme of mutual dependence.

This book is about many of the varied jobs around the world—more specifically about what people are paid for doing them. It considers how attitudes toward the same job can differ from country to country, often reflecting the values and uppermost needs of a society. In addition the incomes of people doing the same or similar jobs in different nations are compared, and in the process some of the harsh facts of economic inequality are illustrated.

Societies have always defined people by the jobs they perform, delineating entirely different roles, attributes, responsibilities, pay and privileges for a banker, for example, than for a bus driver. In examining the economies of nations larger categories—agriculture, manufacturing, the professions—are employed. Another vital category in any analysis of an economy is the number of unemployed; in attempting to understand a country's labor patterns it is essential to know the number of people not working.

Work is also performed by people who are virtual slaves or are so utterly weighed down by the economic constrictions of their existence that they must labor just to survive from one day to the next. There are many, many such people in the world, living in conditions so primitive or remote that they never become part of any analysis. They rarely come to world attention, except when their work no longer produces enough for them to survive and they become victims of famine.

In even moderately affluent societies, most people work not just to survive but to enjoy their lives as well. The amount they earn establishes how much they can spend on the good things of life and defines the importance of their work and therefore their ''worth'' as individuals. It's easy to regard this as a philistine notion, but it is a reality nevertheless. In many societies people's earnings are hardly ever discussed. In fact learning incomes is often taboo, because it's so dangerous; it can lead to envy, resentment and even revolution.

Generally, in countries where information on how much people make is the most guarded, it is because there are stiff taxes to be avoided or because class tensions might ignite if economic injustices were documented. In many European countries, such as France, Italy and West Germany, questions about personal income are considered particularly rude, and yet there is a highly cultivated awareness of how much a job is objectively worth. Major magazines run articles about how much a person should make in the most minute detail, taking into consideration age, number of children, region of employment, level of education and other specific considerations. Such analyses are far more complete and systematic than what is normally found in the United Kingdom or the United States, indicating that the interest is certainly there, although expressed differently.

The book discusses the effects of various forms of taxation in the developed nations and the elaborate measures taken to avoid them. Such devious practices and the countless ways that benefits, prestige and "perks" substitute for direct pay make a completely valid international comparison of salaries very difficult indeed. For example, a jet pilot working for Air India makes about 20% of what his counterpart working for Swissair or Lufthansa earns. Yet the Indian pilot is able to live as well as any other wage earner in India and will probably be provided with excellent living accommodations in the countries he flies to as one of the perks of his job. Although making considerably less money than the German or Swiss pilot, he is much more securely in the elite of his own society due to financial and social benefits that go with his position. Being the captain of a jetliner *means* more in India than in Europe and this reality cannot be expressed in terms of money.

A related problem in comparing incomes in many countries is how to deal with widely divergent standards of living. An income of $10,000 a year in the United States is barely above the poverty line, according to the level set by the federal government; yet it is a veritable fortune in Bangladesh and other developing countries. This must be remembered when viewing the staggering contrasts in income. The sections in this book that illustrate the disparities in the average annual wages for people with the same job in countries with different standards of living also point up the enormous economic disparities between countries.

As international bankers and government officials discovered long ago, there is no ideal way to establish or compare the value of various currencies. Exchange rates between local currencies and the United States dollar fluctuate daily.

Moreover, in the case of some currencies—particularly those of most Communist countries—the official rate ridiculously overstates the value of the local currency and the black market rate understates it. To standardize such data I have used the rates of exchange as reported at the close of business on January 4, 1982 by the *Wall Street Journal* and as reported on January 8, 1982 by the Bank of America NA and SA.

I arbitrarily decided to use the value of each currency on those two days whether the original data were current or, in a few cases, even several years old. This naturally creates some distortion in income values because of fluctuation in exchange rates. It is also important to remember that the dollar has been very strong recently in relation to most other currencies, and therefore local salaries in dollar equivalents will seem lower than they would have been a year ago, or might easily be a year from now. Nevertheless, after receiving a great deal of conflicting advice from experts on how I should calculate exchange rates, I felt this method would make the most sense to the general reader.

Making valid comparisons among many proud countries with widely different levels of economic activity and wealth has proved extraordinarily difficult. Nations are so concerned about just their semantic image that they use a maze of terms to describe themselves: underdeveloped, disadvantaged, relatively less developed, developing but *never* undeveloped. Some countries like to be referred to as relatively least developed, low income developing, even least developed and landlocked. These terms simply refer to levels of poverty, which are best illustrated by the figures for various nations. Both the terms and the figures must be dealt with realistically, as the book attempts to do, drawing on such helpful sources as the International Labor Office.

Another potential pitfall in comparing jobs and salaries in

different countries is that while many jobs are identical all over the world, others sound the same but are actually very different from one country to the next. A world famous movie star or rock performer or opera singer does the same thing in every country and is paid on an international scale. Nuclear physicists, brain surgeons and other highly educated and trained professionals have such unique talents that they can usually move from one place to another whenever they desire, and they know what range of remuneration is available wherever they may go.

The practitioners of many other jobs, however, cannot move easily from country to country. Lawyers are among the most striking examples of this. The jobs that one lawyer in the United States has been trained to perform are done by two in the United Kingdom, four in France, West Germany and Italy—and by no one in many parts of the developing world. This makes a comparison of legal salaries a consuming task; the jobs change in scope from place to place, as do the salaries and prestige of the practitioners. In Japan there are very few lawyers in comparison to the United States, mainly because the Japanese consider this profession of secondary importance and accord it only moderate prestige. In the United States, on the other hand, there are numerous lawyers, and many of them enjoy lucrative and powerful careers.

Despite the challenges and difficulties of comparing what people earn around the globe, some general conclusions can be drawn from this broad study into the world of pay and incomes. Foremost, one is struck to see in actual figures the proof of what is the major problem of the world community; namely, that the developing nations are much poorer than the developed ones, and that there seems to be only faint hope that the situation will be equalized with time. The low incomes for nonagricultural workers in several less developed countries show few signs of rising; indeed they have actually been declining since the oil crisis of 1973-74.

The relatively low incomes in the Communist-bloc countries are more surprising. The workers in a number of the Eastern European countries have higher incomes than their counterparts in the Soviet Union. Poland had the highest wages until the turmoil of the past few years, when inflation and economic decline began to take a terrible toll on the country's standard of living. Currently the labor forces of Czechoslovakia, East Germany and Rumania all enjoy paychecks about twice the size of those in the Soviet Union. As a result Soviet citizens are sometimes confused and resentful when they see people who make more than they do demanding the freedom and economic well-being they themselves do not have.

Developed countries have a number of advantages that may not be immediately apparent. In as basic a matter as gathering data on their own economies, the countries of the European Economic Community, e.g., have such sophisticated information about trends and comparisons among themselves and the other countries of the world that they are aware of numerous policy options which would be unknown in a country like Sri Lanka. On an individual level, the higher the incomes, the more developed the economy and the more job options exist. Most of the discussion of professions is based on what goes on in developed countries. This is not because the developing countries lack these professions, but rather that the number of people trained to practice them is limited and details about their incomes are usually difficult to uncover.

One question always comes up when I discuss this book; how did I find information on a subject of such importance in places where most people do not wish to discuss the topic? When I traveled throughout Europe in search of information about what workers were paid, I received precious little encouragement at first. I was told everywhere that I would learn nothing, that the subject of my research had a bumptious American quality to it, that privacy was sacred on such matters in the more civilized countries of the world.

However, once I made it clear that I was not seeking any one individual's income, but rather the pay for jobs and professions in general, the innate, almost obsessive curiosity about how people are faring economically emerged. To get people to drop their guard, I became a practitioner of the passing question, the indifferent query, the chance expression of puzzlement.

In London, during a pleasant lunch, I asked a barrister about the legal profession in his country and how well it paid. I received a steely glance over a plate of curry. So I asked again, after trying some chutney:

"Would you say that all the barristers in London making more than £150,000 [$289,500] a year would fit into this room?"

"Quite easily," he answered, after checking the dimensions.

"There can't be more than a few dozen of them, then?" I went on.

"At the very most, probably less."

"That's interesting," I observed, "because in America, for better or worse, there are so many lawyers making more than $300,000 a year that they would be crushed into horrible pulp if you tried to get them all into this room."

This exchange appeared to relax his conversational guard and a detailed outline of the legal profession in Britain— with the pay to be earned from bottom to top—followed.

In Paris I vainly sought the salaries of members of the Chamber of Deputies. Talking to a journalist, I said innocently: "It's the strangest thing, but I can't seem to find the salaries of deputies. In England and America that sort of thing is public knowledge. The money, after all, does come from the taxpayer's pocket.''

"Of course it's public information in France. We are a democracy and these facts must be available to every citizen. We'll go down to the government information office right now and find out.'' Alas, after searching through thick volumes of official documents, they did not have the information. Everyone was very embarrassed.

"Then we'll go to the Chamber and ask directly,'' my journalist friend said. We did, and met an imperious and extremely correct official who knew what she was about.

"And why do you want this information?'' she asked my friend.

"It's public information isn't it. Surely? My American colleague is doing research on the subject.''

"Ah, so that's it,'' she said, looking me over. ''You are probably financed by an American foundation to do research on the government? Is that it?'' She asked in a tone that implied that most Americans she met were financed by foundations.

"Well, you might say so,'' I answered weakly.

"In that case I will give you the information—because of your research,'' she emphasized, glancing at my journalist friend to make sure he understood the drift of things. In any case, I got the information and we both got the point that public information is what the government decides it is.

Another conversation illustrated the importance of keeping incomes secret to avoid problems with the tax authorities. In Brussels I was told that the more successful a person is the more he had a need and a right to employ every conceivable means to avoid paying taxes.

"Take the president of my bank, for instance. I don't know how much he really makes and you can be sure that the government doesn't either. If either of us did, it would mean to me that he isn't a very clever businessman after all,'' I was informed with a proud smile.

"But it's your money, along with that of others, he is paying himself with. Doesn't that make you nervous?" I asked.

"Well, it might, but I know him and trust him. I certainly don't trust the government. In fact, if someone cheats me, I would feel much better if it were my banker than the tax bureau.'' Such is the attitude that makes tax evasion a positive thing, and an activity that brings the citizens together in a conspiracy against government.

Scrutinizing magazines, newspapers, official journals, government reports, public documents; conducting official and unofficial interviews; reading between the lines of answers or reactions to many questions—all of these and more I have used in assembling this book. I am grateful for the assistance of many people in its preparation; there are far too many to name but I thank everyone who helped.

Michael Claes of Hill and Knowlton opened many doors for me, as did Elly Pick-Jacobs and Philippe Biebuyck of Manpower, Inc. I also wish to thank Charles Evans and Richard Harris of Bentley and Evans for their advice and introductions to knowledgeable people in Europe. Daniel Porot was very helpful in Switzerland and I am grateful to Richard Bolles for arranging several important meetings for me. I would like to express my gratitude to William Nitze for the great amount of information and insight he gave me and to Marcus Weiner, who was also most helpful. Kerrie Buitrago at the European Community office in New York was a source of much information and research data.

Edward Knappman has remained my editor and publisher for this book as he was for my previous one, something which from time to time has tried his great patience and skill, but our relationship has been invaluable to me and his advice has done a great deal toward shaping this volume. Joseph Reilly once again did a superb copy editing job on the manuscript and the painstaking care and imagination with which he tackled this task will never be forgotten. Angela Amoroso spent many long evenings typing the manuscript after deciphering it as only she can, and she was invaluable. As they say, the errors are mine.

1

INTERNATIONAL ORGANIZATIONS

There are literally hundreds of international organizations, ranging from the United Nations to the International Weightlifting Federation. It is generally agreed that the nations which are members of these groups get the kind of organization they deserve because of what they put into them in time, effort and money. However, there is considerable disagreement about whether the people who work for the major world organizations get the salaries they deserve, whether they get more or whether they get less.

The International Weightlifting Federation, headquartered in Budapest, is financed by fees from participants at international events, and the salaries of its 17-member bureau are minimal. The United Nations, with headquarters in New York, is financed by contributions from member nations. Javier Perez de Cuellar, the secretary general of the United Nations, receives a gross salary of $158,340 plus $16,000 for expenses, $22,000 for "hospitality," $40,000 for travel and either a free residence in New York or $25,000 toward establishment of his own residence. This comes to $236,000 (without the residence allowance), making him the second highest paid political leader in the world after President Ronald Reagan.

Under the direction of the secretary general an international civil service administers the worldwide operations of the United Nations. The organization, with its 15,000 employees in New York City, Geneva and elsewhere around the globe, expended a budget of $1,247,000,000 in 1980-81. The amount of money United Nations civil servants earn is based on the salaries of the best paid national civil servants from among the contributing member states. During the 1970s the pay scales of civil service workers in the United States were emulated, but since the relative decline in pay for those workers, the United Nations has used the civil service salary scales of other countries as a benchmark.

At the top of the United Nations civil service are 32 undersecretary generals (equivalent to permanent secretaries in the United Kingdom), each of whom earns a gross annual salary of $96,765; and 52 assistant secretary generals (equivalent to permanent undersecretaries in the United Kingdom), each of whom makes $85,864 per year.

Below the level of undersecretary general and assistant secretary general are "directors" (D2) and "principal officers" (D1), followed by five categories of professional employees (P5 to P1), who in theory are the equivalent of foreign service officers. The starting salary in 1981 for the lowest step in the lowest rank of these categories (P1) was $18,208 per year, which is higher than the starting salary for a foreign service officer in most all nations.

These five categories of professional employees comprise the backbone of the United Nations' civil service staff. They include program officers, bureau chiefs, department heads, administrative controllers, supervisors, operations officers, analysts and others needed to staff an extensive bureaucracy. Also among these ranks are translators and interpreters, an essential component of the multilanguage organization. They must have an expert knowledge of at least three of the organization's official languages, which are Arabic, Chinese, English, French, Spanish and Russian. Interpreters start at P-2, earning $24,233 a year, to P-3, making $43,375 a year at highest level in grade. Opportunities exist for specially competent people to go as high as P-5, with a salary of $61,231 a year at the highest level in grade. (The lower positions at U.N. headquarters and offices in the field, such as secretaries, clerks, etc., are paid on a different schedule; an effort is made to keep their salaries competitive with local conditions.)

The same pay scales apply to professional employees of the United Nations' 23 specialized agencies, including the International Labor Organization (ILO), the International Monetary Fund (IMF), the General Agreement on Tariffs and Trade (GATT), the United Nations Educational, Scientific and Cultural Organization (UNESCO) and the World Health Organization (WHO), to name a few of the best known. Some countries are rumored to supplement the salaries of their nationals who are civil service employees of the United Nations, and other countries, particularly members of the Communist bloc, are understood to take part of the salaries of their nationals who work for the United Nations while providing them with housing. (In view of the fact that a Chinese senior minister is paid about 400 yuan [$228] a month, or about 4,800 yuan [$2,736] a year, the annual salary of $96,765 that he would make as an undersecretary general represents a raise of monumental proportions and an assessment by his government would be understandable.)

While all the agencies have the same salary pattern, some have perks that set them off from others. The IMF has about 1,500 employees, many of whom live in the Washington, D.C. area. They have the privilege of being able to join the

Bretton Woods Recreation Center, which was originally created for employees of the agency because of the prejudices of certain clubs and recreational facilities in the D.C. area. The center is a country club of sorts, with a swimming pool, golf course, tennis courts, restaurant and many social activities. Membership is now available, on a very exclusive basis, to employees of the World Bank, the Inter-American Bank and some other members of the international banking fraternity. The existence of the center aggravates many who regard it as a symbol of the elite character of the international finance community, but the members cherish it as one of their favorite fringe benefits.

All U.N. professional employees receive education allowances for their children up to about $4,000 a year and cost-of-living adjustments based on their rank and marital status. For example, an undersecretary general in New York with dependents can receive an adjustment of $454.19 a month. However, an assessment is taken from the salaries of all professional employees at the United Nations' headquarters in New York. This assessment, which is calculated on roughly the same basis as U.S. income tax, is used by the organization to pay for administrative and other expenses.

Other fringe benefits include a housing allowance and a repatriation grant, which is determined according to length of service and rank at the time of retirement. In addition employees of the United Nations and its agencies receive generous travel arrangements for both business and vacation trips, sometimes allowing extensive indirect routing for the convenience of the employee. Home leave is substantial and certain advantages can be taken because of the diplomatic classification afforded to U.N. personnel.

The salaries and benefits at the United Nations are a source of much criticism, just as the benefits given to diplomatic personnel in all countries are generally objects of resentment. But the image of the United Nations as an ineffective organization makes its pay scales and perks all the more irritating. One particular sore point is that despite the goal of salary parity with the highest paying member state, the first 84 people under the secretary general (32 undersecretary generals and 52 assistant secretary generals) all make more than the highest ranking civil servant in any country in the world.

The organization's hiring practices have also been the subject of considerable controversy. All professional jobs below the level of assistant secretary general are filled according to a national quota system that is based on several factors, including a country's budget contribution as a percentage of the total U.N. budget. According to this system, the United States is awarded from 381 to 516 professional positions and the USSR from 171 to 232, although neither of the two countries fills all the posts awarded. On the other hand, Togo is entitled to fill two to seven posts and fills seven, and Algeria is entitled to four to nine positions and fills 17. The desire of certain U.N. missions to enlarge their staffs, hire political friends, freeze out enemies and so on has caused considerable infighting, and although such infighting is common among employees of all bureaucracies, none are as much in the public eye or, on the average, as highly paid as the employees of the United Nations.

U.N. agencies also come under fire when they do not fulfill their functions in the eyes of the nations that either support them or are affected by their activities or both. UNDRA (United Nations Disaster Relief Office), headquartered in Geneva, is charged with arranging cooperation among relief agencies and refugee organizations in times of major disasters. An inspection team recently found that the agency had had its budget increased from $330,000 to $3.6 million and its staff from six to 50. The agency, which is directed by a secretary general earning $96,765, has been the target of much criticism since 1980. At that time, despite its explosion in staff and funds, it had taken part in less than half of the disaster relief operations mounted around the world.

As president of the World Bank for Reconstruction and Development, Robert McNamara made $148,000 a year before retiring in 1981. His successor, A. W. Clausen, currently earns about $150,000 a year (he has told people that he voluntarily accepted a salary cut of about $600,000 when he left his job as president of BankAmerica Corporation to become head of the World Bank).

Although closely guarded secrets, the salaries and benefits of members of the Board of Governors and executive directors and assistant executive directors at the World Bank are generally equivalent to those at the top of the U.N. structure. At one time the paychecks and perks of World Bank employees were probably the most generous in the world of international organizations, but this is no longer so true. Promotions are still based on merit, more than in almost any other international body with the exception of the IMF and the European Community. Stipulations that the United States has attached to grants of funds to the bank, which represent between one-fifth and one-quarter of its total assets, state that the U.S. executive director may receive a salary no greater than $61,300 and the U.S. assistant executive director no more than $59,119. It is certain that most of the 18 or so other executive directors are paid higher salaries than the U.S. executive director.

Many of the international organizations that abound in the world have very specific regional interests. For example, the International Moselle Company consists of representatives from France, Luxembourg and West Germany who are charged with overseeing the maintenance of canalization in the Moselle River to facilitate inland water traffic between the three countries. The company is funded by the three countries. There are many similar organizations made up of representatives from separate sovereign states cooperating for a mutual purpose, be it commerce, trade, sport, culture, art, politics, defense.

The European Community is possibly the most important of these organizations. It comprises the European Economic Community, the European Coal and Steel Community and the European Atomic Energy Community. The organization represents the efforts of 10 Western European nations (Belgium, Denmark, France, West Germany, Greece, Ireland, Italy, Luxembourg, the Netherlands and the United Kingdom) to cohere the often diverse economic and political interests of an area of the world where nationalism and strife have been the normal state of affairs for centuries.

Among the chief institutions of the European Community are the Commission, consisting of 13 members, each of whom serves a four-year term, and a president and five vice presidents, who are eligible to serve two two-year terms; the Council of Ministers, who are appointed by the individual member nations; and the European Parliament, made up of members delegated by the national parliaments. In addition the heads of state of the member nations meet three times a year. The organization has a number of operating groups, such as the Customs Union and the European Monetary System, that are staffed by civil servants. Its 1981-82 budget is about $26 billion.

There have been numerous scathing commentaries in the major European countries during the past few years over the salaries that the European Community pays its civil servants. Such outrage is quite extraordinary among people generally so blase or cynical about the paychecks of politicians ("What difference does it make what they are paid? They steal the rest," is a common remark). While not really

7

known by many people, the salaries of European Community employees are assumed to be enormous.

Actually the salary schedules for employees of the European Community are remarkably similar to those of the U.N. system except that the tax on salaries is computed on a less inclusive basis and is smaller in total than that levied by the United Nations. The Community's salaries are somewhat larger and its fringe benefits, such as education grants, housing, post adjustments etc., are slightly more generous.

The gross annual salary of President Gaston Egmont Thorn, which is less than that of the U.N. secretary general, is 4,886,674 Belgian francs ($146,600); vice presidents of the Commission receive an annual salary of 4,426,337 Belgian francs ($132,790); and the annual salary of regular members of the Commission is 3,983,703 Belgian francs ($119,511). The highest ranking civil service grade at the highest step, A1/6, is paid approximately 3,760,417 Belgian francs ($98,363), or slightly more than the salary of an undersecretary general at the United Nations.

The members of the European Parliament are paid according to the salaries of their national parliaments. The number of members, over 400, and the body's relative lack of power have made it the object of much scorn. A CBS "60 Minutes" report launched an extremely shallow and biased attack on the Parliament in 1981, calling it the "gravy train." The report claimed that since all the minutes of the Parliament had to be translated into all the languages of its members, every word spoken amounted to $25 in translation, transcription and publication costs. Such stories have done little to endear the community to European taxpayers. However, the European Community's growing economic and political role is a force of history and will ultimately outweigh the unpopularity of its civil service salaries and benefits.

Whether the prestige of the United Nations will ever grow

to match the size of its salaries is a different question. So far the organization's accomplishments have appeared to the average citizen of most countries to be largely a sham and its immense physical plant, both in New York and Geneva, has been a source of aggravation. Yet the organization has only the power invested in it by the members, and that is very little indeed. Its main burden has been to bear the brunt of outrage and mockery from states whose purposes were not aided by it.

Without real power, high salaries become offensive. When an undersecretary who earns $96,765 as coordinator of disaster relief cannot effectively relieve disasters, he not surprisingly comes under attack, perhaps unfairly if the constraints put upon him by member states became publicly known.

In Geneva the Palais des Nations, the headquarters of many of the U.N. agencies, is located in a beautiful setting with Mont Blanc visible in the background, offering a serenity and confidence to the tourist groups that trundle through. The International Labor Office building there is an immense, stunning structure, filled with half-empty meeting halls and offices where many well-paid employees produce labor studies of genuine value to the developed and, particularly, the developing countries.

But knowing that the total payroll for these thousands of employees is probably greater than that for the foreign ministers of all the countries of the world put together raises certain doubts. Is this a case where generous salaries, splendid benefits and a superb setting are merely expensive covering for cracks in the foundation of the whole enterprise?

2

NATIONAL GOVERNMENTS

Prime Minister George Price of Belize, one of the world's smallest and newest independent countries, earns about $8,000 a year, drives an old Land Rover and lives in a tiny bungalow provided by his government. His counterpart in the People's Republic of China is Prime Minister Zhao Ziyang, who receives an official salary of 560 yuan (about $319) per month, or 6,720 yuan ($3,820) a year, plus benefits, including limousines, housing, special travel arrangements, official expenses and other comforts that put him in a class far higher than his salary indicates. His famous predecessor, Mao Zedong, enjoyed the luxury of a $4 million villa, complete with swimming pool, and traveled in such munificence that his life style became a popular rallying point for attacks on him after his death.

Switzerland, another relatively small country, is governed by a Federal Council consisting of seven members, each of whom earns 203,000 Swiss francs ($113,680). One of the seven (Fritz Honegger for 1982) is chosen president and receives a salary of 215,000 Swiss francs ($120,400). In the United States, which is roughly equivalent in geographical size to China, President Ronald Reagan earns $200,000 a year and receives a $40,000 nontaxable travel allotment and a $50,000 taxable expense account. In addition President Reagan has all manner of transportation, including limousines, helicopters, ships and a huge jet aircraft, at his personal disposal. He dwells for free in a finely lit mansion, recently appointed with exquisite china and beautiful antiques, he has bands to play for him, artists to sing and dance for him and practically anything else he might desire in the way of entertainment or recreation for himself and his large official staff.

These opposite ends of the salary spectrum for world leaders do not indicate the degree of power and influence each holds. Although Prime Minister Price earns over twice the salary of Prime Minister Zhao, he does not wield an iota of his power. Nor does the salary of the president of the Federal Council of Switzerland, as financially powerful and wealthy as that country is, reflect political authority greater than Zhao's or President Reagan's. In fact the salary of the president of the United States, while the highest of elected politicians in the world, is low when measured against that of thousands of business executives, lawyers, doctors, entertainers, criminals and others.

Executive and Legislative Services

To track down the earnings of world leaders and principal politicians is to follow a slippery and often treacherous path. Figures for leaders and politicians in most nations are not available, not to researchers, journalists or citizen-taxpayers. This is particularly the case in authoritarian and totalitarian countries, as in China, where a stated salary is at best an ideological statistic designed to give the appearance of equality. The same is true in all Communist countries, and whenever a government minister's salary is given, it means little unless the real scope of benefits and subtle perks are known. In China, as in many other Communist states, preferred educational opportunities at home and abroad go to the children of those in power. (Over one-half of the Chinese students who first came to the United States were offspring of high officials.) Greater travel freedom, superior and more private living accommodations, and better quality food and other essentials are reserved for the higher ranges of officialdom.

In dictatorships, which exist in one form or another in well over half of the nations of the world, the real salary for the head man is rarely ever known and frequently does not exist in any formal sense. Payments to politicians and officials often come not only from public funds but also from bribes, intricate systems of patronage, favors for sale, confiscatory taxes, involuntary tithes and so on down to sanctioned brigandage. In the most severe dictatorships the sums of money paid to the leadership are kept very secret, and the methods used to obtain them are often crude, distasteful and violent.

To any reasonably sophisticated citizen of these countries, the question of how much the political leader makes would seem laughable. What could be more comical than asking how much was the annual salary of the late General Anastasio Somoza of Nicaragua, famous for, among his other fiscal innovations, his expropriation of earthquake relief money? What is the paycheck of General Alfredo Stroessner of Paraguay; of President Sese Mobutu of Zaire, whose awesome system of bribery extends throughout the country; of President Saddam Hussein of Iraq or President Muhammad Zia-ul-Haq of Pakistan?

The countries where information on the salaries of government officials, both elected and appointed, is available are generally those where the electorate selects the leaders and independent legislative bodies have control over the finances of the state. The following list presents the salaries of political leaders, ministers and, if available, members of representative bodies in a selected group of these countries. All of them except China are ruled by some form of democracy, be it directly elected, limited or parliamentary, and most, but not all, are developed countries.

Australia	Prime Minister Malcolm Fraser receives a salary of A$104,348 ($117,913); Deputy Prime Minister J. Douglas Anthony earns A$81,981 ($92,638) per year; cabinet members earn A$69,165 ($78,156) per year; noncabinet ministers earn A$66,185 ($74,789) per year; backbenchers earn A$45,063 ($50,921) per year.
Belgium	Deputies and senators receive an annual salary of 900,000 Belgian francs ($27,000); both are entitled to free transportation and some official expense allowances.
Canada	Prime Minister Pierre Trudeau receives a salary of C$64,000 ($53,760) per year; cabinet ministers and the leader of the opposition earn C$48,000 ($40,320) per year. Members of Parliament get a sessional allowance of C$28,000 ($24,024) per year plus various expense and travel allowances.

China

Prime Minister Zhao Ziyang receives a salary of 560 yuan ($319) per month, or 6,720 yuan ($3,828) per year; vice chairmen, deputy prime ministers and other ministers earn from 250 yuan to 400 yuan ($143 to $228) per month, or 3,000 yuan to 4,800 yuan ($1,716 to $2,736) per year.

France

President Francois Mitterand receives a salary of approximately 511,200 francs ($90,000) per year. Members of Parliament earn 23,000 francs ($4,140) per month with 2.5 to four additional months pay because they are in a special civil service category known as *hors echelle* ("outside the ladder," or outside the normal pay scales), making their actual salary approximately 335,000 francs ($60,300) a year; in addition they receive expense allowances for travel, official duties and office support.

Germany, West

Chancellor Helmut Schmidt receives a salary of approximately 280,000 marks ($126,000) per year plus expenses; members of the Federal Diet earn approximately 182,000 marks ($81,900) per year, including expenses.

India

Prime Minister Indira Gandhi and other ministers of the cabinet receive 27,000 rupees ($3,000) per year;

deputy ministers earn 21,000 rupees ($2,333) per year. All ministers are entitled to free use of furnished residences and transportation and official expense allowances.

Italy

President Alessandro Pertini receives a salary of 30 million lire ($24,000) per year, 180 million lire ($144,000) in special funds, 292 million lire ($233,600) for the Office of Secretary General and Secretariat personnel, and 100 million lire ($80,000) for maintenance of presidential properties. In addition to their pay as deputies or senators, Prime Minister Giovanni Spadolini and other ministers of state earn 6,174,810 lire ($4,940) a year, based on 13 months and including allowances. Deputies and senators are paid 36,075,000 lire ($28,860) per year and receive free transportation, telephone and barbering services, and while they must pay for their own bar and cafe privileges, the prices are lower than on the street.

Japan

Prime Minister Zenko Suzuki receives 1,550,000 yen ($7,130) per month, or 20,150,000 yen ($92,690) per year, (based on 13 months), plus expenses, housing and transportation; cabinet members earn 1,130,000 yen ($5,198) per month, or 14,690,000 yen ($67,574) per year (based on 13 months), plus expenses, housing and transportation.

New Zealand Prime Minister Robert Muldoon receives a salary of NZ$60,091 ($49,876) per year plus housing and a tax-free expense account of NZ$10,725 ($8,902) per year. Ministers with portfolio earn NZ$41,456 ($34,408) per year plus tax-free expense allowances; all ministers are entitled to NZ$44 ($36.52) per day while traveling on business within New Zealand. Members of the House of Representatives earn NZ$24,326 ($20,190) per year plus expense accounts varying from NZ$5,590 to NZ$8,500 ($4,640 to $7,055) according to area of electorate represented.

South Africa Prime Minister Pieter Willem Botha receives a salary of 43,000 rand ($45,150) per year plus a reimbursive allowance of 20,000 rand ($21,000); members of the cabinet earn 23,500 rand ($24,675) per year plus a reimbursive allowance of 6,500 rand ($6,825); deputy ministers earn 19,000 rand ($19,950) per year plus the same reimbursive allowance as cabinet members.

Sri Lanka President Junius R. Jayawardene receives a tax-free salary of 5,000 rupees ($243) per year plus housing,

17

Sweden

United Kingdom

United States

transportation and expense allowances for maintenance of his office.
In a complex system of subventions, each seat in the Federal Diet received 115,000 kronor ($20,700) as of the last official statement (1978), which amounted to an annual salary for members.
Prime Minister Margaret Thatcher is entitled to an annual salary of £36,725 ($70,879), of which she draws £27,825 ($53,702). Lord Hailsham, the Lord Chief Justice, Lord Chancellor, is entitled to an annual salary of £44,500 ($85,885), of which he draws £27,885 ($53,818). Cabinet ministers earn £27,825 ($53,702) per year and receive a secretarial allowance of £4,600 ($8,878), a living allowance of £3,886 ($7,500) and travel expenses between London and their permanent place of residence. Members of Parliament earn £13,950 ($26,924) per year and receive the same additional stipends and expense allowances as ministers.
President Ronald Reagan receives a salary of $200,000 per year plus a $40,000 tax-free allowance for travel and entertainment and a $50,000 taxable allowance for defrayment of expenses related to official duties. Vice President George Bush earns

$84,700 per year plus a $10,000 taxable allowance for expenses. Members of the cabinet earn $69,630 per year and receive transportation and limited expense allowances. Members of Congress earn $60,663 per year and receive a $6,500 taxable allowance for expenses; in addition they have the right to earn outside income up to $25,000 a year and their living expenses while in Washington, D.C. are tax-deductible.

Monarchy

In the United Kingdom and other countries the legislature provides an annual sum for the personal and household expenses of the monarch. Known as the civil list, this sum is often the source of vigorous and vitriolic debate. Frequently no amount is made public. The following civil lists are public information.

Sweden 8.2 million kronor ($1,476,000), which does not include funds for maintenance of the royal palaces.

United Kingdom In 1981 the Civil List of the Queen was £3,964,000 ($7,650,520), which included annuities of £286,000 ($551,980) for Queen Elizabeth, the Queen Mother; £166,000 ($320,380) for Princess Anne; and £98,000

($189,140) for Princess Margaret. Each year the state also contributes £5,699,912 ($11,000,830) for the upkeep of the royal palaces and £11,635,000 ($22,455,550) for running costs and maintenance of the royal yacht, the royal train and whatever other means of travel are necessary. The civil list is tax free.

In addition royal families have their own incomes from private estates, rents from land holdings and other sources, such as investments. Some of this money is often paid to the state, but not always. The inherited fortune of the royal family of the United Kingdom is estimated to be worth approximately £70 million ($140 million), and it is passed from monarch to monarch. Part of the interest derived from this money defrays official expenses. Currently, for example, Prince Charles gives the Treasury one-half of the net profits from his rents and other income from the Duchy of Cornwall. This amounted to more than £250,000 ($500,000) given to the government in 1981.

Civil Service

The power and prestige of the government and its ability to act effectively depends to a large degree on the civil service establishment, whether called that or the party apparatus or the national cadre or any of a number of other identifications. The civil service is the professional, relatively unchanging body of policy administrators that makes government function or not function, depending on the country.

It is easy to appreciate the enormous importance of the civil service, considering the number of responsibilities that a central government may have: defense, education, health, welfare, transportation, foreign affairs, justice, law enforcement, compilation and distribution of information and statistics, immigration and emigration, currency and banking, customs, railways and air traffic, state industrial enterprises (in part or totally), administration of local authority in regions, districts, communalities and municipalities and many other activities.

In many countries all of the above and more are under the control of the central government. The percentage of GNP spent by central governments, which varies a great deal from country to country, is an interesting indicator of the extent of political and economic power held by governments. This spending includes as a major item the civil service payroll, which can be a huge factor in a nation's economic budget.

The following list shows the total outlays by governments of selected developed nations as a percentage of GNP for the year 1978. The countries are ranked from the highest spending to the lowest.

The table shows the range in the size of the role that governments play in their economies; Sweden spends nearly twice as much proportionately as Switzerland, Japan, Australia, and the United States, for example. Yet while civil servants and other government employees may be relatively more numerous in Sweden, they do not necessarily have more prestige than their counterparts in either countries. Often the larger the governmental bureaucracy the more a focus of criticism and controversy it is. This is especially true of the amount civil servants are paid, which is an ongoing source of political friction in most Western democracies, particularly the United Kingdom and the United States.

TOTAL GOVERNMENT OUTLAY
AS PERCENTAGE OF GNP (1978)

Country	Percent
Sweden	59.7
Netherlands	57.5
Norway	52.3
Belgium	49.1
Germany, West	46.5
Italy	46.3
France	45.2
United Kingdom	43.6
Canada	40.9
Finland	39.1
United States	33.4
Australia	32.1
Japan	31.1
Switzerland	30.1
Spain	29.0

Source: *OECD Economic Outlook*, no. 29, July 1981.

In the United Kingdom the head of the Home Civil Service, Sir Ian Bancroft, receives an annual salary of £35,845 ($69,181), which is more than the salary of the highest paid U.S. civil servant, who makes $64,600 a year. This is virtually the only example of a British official being paid more than his American counterpart and, to a large degree, is the result of a pay limit that has been placed on U.S. government workers' salaries by the past two administrations. Currently many employees at different levels of responsibility are receiving the same pay due to the freeze.

In the United Kingdom a permanent secretary, the country's highest ranking civil servant, earns £33,170 ($64,018) per year; his equivalent in West Germany, a *Staatssekretar* ("state secretary"), earns 13,156 marks ($5,920) per month for a 13-month year, or 171,028 marks ($76,963) a year, which is somewhat higher than the Englishman's pay. All civil service jobs have complex benefits that depend on many differing factors; for purposes of standardization only the base salary is given here. In France the highest pay grade in the civil service, within the top category known as *hors echelle,* is that of a bureau chief or director general; it ranges from approximately 12,000 francs to 19,100 francs ($2,160 to $3,438) per month. The annual salary, equivalent to 14 or 14.5 months' pay, is from 168,000 to 276,900 francs ($30,240 to $49,858). (The number of people in the category *hors echelle* and their exact pay are not made public.)

In Italy the highest salary for a director general and those with equivalent responsibility is from 14 million lire to 21.5 million lire ($11,200 to $17,200) a year net with a complex benefits system based on many factors, including length of service. The benefits and perks of government workers in Italy are crucially important, especially when comparing their base annual salaries to those of government employees in other developed countries. In Canada the top-level pay in the civil service is C$50,000 ($42,000), with a very few making higher.

At the other end of the pay scale in these countries, a junior officer in the British civil service can earn about £4,766 to £5,700 ($9,198 to $11,001) a year, compared with about $9,000 a year in the United States, about 24,000 marks ($10,800) a year in West Germany, about 30,000 francs ($5,400) a year with considerable additional fringe benefits in France, 7.2 million lire ($5,760) a year in Italy and C$9,500 to C$10,000 ($7,980 to $8,400) a year in Canada.

The official base salary of section chiefs and managerial and administrative staff in China ranges from 108 yuan to 190 yuan ($62 to $108) per month, or 1,296 yuan to 2,280 yuan ($744 to $1,296) a year. Office staff earn 50 yuan to 60 yuan ($29 to $34) per month, or 600 yuan to 720 yuan ($348 to $408) a year. In the Australian civil service, professional officers and permanent secretaries, the highest grade, earn from A$56,000 to A$60,000 ($63,280 to $67,800) per year. The entry level in the category below is about A$8,000 ($9,040) a year.

Foreign and Diplomatic Service

In most countries the foreign service is related to the civil service, but its organization and pay structure are often independent. Generally countries do not make public the pay of their diplomatic personnel, and the complexity of the allowances, benefits, subsidies and expense funds varies so greatly from country to country that it is almost impossible to determine a realistic base figure. Also the salary depends greatly on the country to which a diplomat has been assigned.

The annual base salary for an ambassador of the Italian government is from 14,000,000 lire to 21,560,000 lire ($11,200 to $17,248). The Japanese ambassador to the United States makes 660,000 yen ($2,970) per month in salary plus 645,000 yen ($2,903) per month in expenses and allowances, or 1,305,000 yen ($5,873) per month; his annual income is 16,965,000 yen ($76,343). The Japanese ambassador to the United Kingdom makes 810,000 yen ($3,645) per month in salary plus 600,000 yen ($2,700) per month in expenses, or 1,410,000 yen (6,345) per month; his annual income is 18,330,000 yen ($82,485). The United States pays its ambassadors from $50,112 to $60,663 depending upon the category of the post. Ambassadors of the Australian government earn from A$38,000 to A$60,000 ($42,940 to $67,800) per year depending upon the post; salaries for Canadian ambassadors range from C$40,000 to C$50,000 ($33,600 to $42,000) and higher for some posts. In both countries the foreign service is part of the civil service.

The Military

The pay scales within a country's military organization often reflect the standard of living in that country. However, the prestige attached to a tour or a career in the military often bears little relation to the commensurate salary. The chief of staff of the Indian Army earns $5,795 a year, and a recruit in the same army receives only $21.59 a month, or $259.08 a year. Yet the Indian Army is recognized as one of the best trained and motivated in the world, and for every recruit admitted there are seven or eight rejected. Recruits are enlisted for a tour of 17 years and officers for life. This remarkable longevity of service, reminiscent of the Roman legions, adds to the efficiency, esprit and prestige of the Indian Army, which provides a good example of an area where the value of a job cannot be measured simply in money.

The following table compares salaries at four levels in selected armies. These figures are the latest available for 1981; it must be remembered that military pay is constantly subject to revision and alteration.

The difference in military pay scales is quite extraordinary and, considering standards of living, the United States is surprisingly low in relation to certain other countries. However, Congress has passed a pay increase for members of the U.S. armed forces and it was signed into law in December 1981. One striking disparity is that a general in the Portuguese Army earns less than a private in most of the other services listed.

Another noteworthy feature of this comparison is the much higher salaries paid to the military in Canada and Australia. A private soldier in the Australian Army, for example, makes about 55 times as much as his counterpart in the Indian Army.

SELECTED MILITARY PAY SCALES IN 11 COUNTRIES (1981)

	General Local Currency	General U.S. $ Equivalent	Major* Local Currency	Major* U.S. $ Equivalent	Sergeant Local Currency	Sergeant U.S. $ Equivalent	Private** Local Currency	Private** U.S. $ Equivalent
Australia	A$ 52,000	$58,160	A$ 26,500	$29,945	NA		A$ 14,300	$16,160
Belgium	BF 1,161,120	$34,834	BF 934,800	$28,044	BF 422,142	$12,664	BF 301,765	$ 9,053
Canada	NA		C$ 40,470	$33,995	C$ 25,044	$21,036	C$ 18,720	$15,724
Germany, West***	DM 114,686	$51,609	DM 34,892	$15,701	DM 24,271	$10,921	DM 15,249	$ 6,862
Greece	Dr 2,065,401	$36,140	Dr 1,479,213	$25,883	Dr 658,254	$11,518	Dr 460,629	$ 8,060
Italy	Lira 24,200,000	$19,360	Lira 12,500,000	$10,000	Lira 8,021,000	$ 6,417	Lira 754,000	$ 6,032
Netherlands	DG 97,487	$39,970	DG 52,000	$21,320	DG 31,485	$12,909	DG 23,270	$ 9,540
Portugal	Esc 373,712	$ 5,723	Esc 322,778	$ 4,943	Esc 177,224	$ 2,714	Esc 18,937	$ 290
Turkey	NA		TL 4,700,000	$35,100	TL 2,555,000	$19,110	TL 521,040	$ 3,900
United Kingdom	£ 33,170	$64,018	£ 11,304	$21,816	£ 6,986	$13,483	£ 4,084	$ 7,882
			-13,494	-26,043	-8,025	-15,488	-6,085	-11,744
United States	$ 45,528	—	$ 20,832	—	$ 9,262	—	$ 5,375	—

Source: NATO and interviews, articles, reports, information from the governments.
Note: Currency equivalents are as of 1982.

*No figures were available for a major in the Canadian, West German or Italian armies; the figures supplied are for a lieutenant colonel in the Canadian Army, a captain in the West German Army and a colonel in the Italian Army.

**In the case of Belgium, West Germany, Greece, Italy and Turkey, the figures supplied are for a "soldier," which is roughly the equivalent of private. In the case of the Netherlands the figure is for a recruit.

***All salaries are based on 10 years of service.

Local Government

Many important jobs, including that of police officer, which are the responsibility of local governments in the United Kingdom and the United States, to name two prominent examples, come under the national civil service in other countries. In the United Kingdom there are over 50 police authorities. The average British constable's pay with overtime is about £7,384 ($14,251), and while pay is negotiated nationally, each authority governs its own police force.

In West Germany, where the average annual salary for a police officer was about 34,112 marks ($15,350) in 1980-81, officers are hired, paid and promoted within the regular schedule of civil service jobs under a standardized police law for all federal states. Their employment status is the same as that of other government bureaucrats and armed service personnel. A similar system exists in France, where an inspector in Paris begins at 50,388 francs ($9,070) and can earn as much as 117,585 francs ($21,165) per year before retirement.

Italy has several police forces. In addition to the 85,000-man Carabinieri, whose junior officers, equivalent to corporals in the army, earned annual salaries of 8,710,000 lire ($6,968) in 1980, there are five other police forces: the Police Security Guard; the Finance Guard; a paramilitary force entrusted with border security; the Municipal Police Forces established to handle traffic and enforce municipal regulations; and the Secret Service, which, along with the Carabinieri, is assigned to fight terrorism, principally the infamous Red Brigades. (In addition the Public Security Guard has an antiterrorist subunit, called *Digos.*) The pay scales of these forces are generally equivalent to those of the Carabinieri, although some salaries are kept secret.

27

In the United States, municipal and state police forces are under the control of local governments, and salaries of police officers vary from region to region and city to city. In New York City in 1980-81 the pay scale for police officers, who are municipal employees, ranged from $18,000 for junior officers to $45,000 a year, and in some cases more, for senior officers. In Canada regional and municipal police constables are almost as well paid. In 1982 the salary for a constable was C$20,071 ($16,860), rising to C$29,071 ($24,420) after three years; a sergeant with 10 years on the job earned C$32,931 ($27,662). Constables in Canada's national police force, the Royal Canadian Mounted Police, earn an average of C$27,400 ($23,016).

Firefighters in all the countries mentioned make slightly less than police officers. However, in the United Kingdom, where the average pay for a firefighter is £6,136 ($11,842), they make considerably less. Firemen in the United States and Canada have attained virtual parity with police officers, which is the trend in most developed countries.

A mayor of a city in France with 400,000 inhabitants or more can earn as high as 214,097 francs ($38,537), which is well below that of Mayor Edward Koch of New York City, whose salary of $80,000 a year makes him the highest paid mayor in the world. Running close to the mayor of New York is the administrator of Vancouver, British Columbia, who earns $69,456 per year.

There are special areas of local government in all countries, some passed down by tradition, others created by constitutional design. Their number and variety are infinite, and in the countries where local autonomy and custom are strong, there is often much friction between these local bodies and the federal authorities. However, in a world constantly becoming more compact both economically and politically, the role of national government generally appears to be increasing, welcome or not. Whether we speak of the huge public sector in newly independent nations or the expansion of established civil bureaucracies in developed countries, one of the great problems of this decade will be how to deal with the enormous cost of government payrolls.

So overwhelming is the cost of paying for huge central governments that the debts piling up threaten the continuing viability of many economies. For example, in the United States the unfunded liability for federal pension plans is over $900 billion and is growing annually. With this specter hanging over the head of one of the world's strongest economies, it is easy to imagine the financial dilemmas caused by uncontrolled government expenditures—prominently including salaries and benefits—confronting numerous other nations.

3

MULTINATIONAL CORPORATIONS

In the United States alone at least nine major management consulting firms regularly conduct studies to advise multinational corporations on appropriate pay scales for the employees they send to their affiliates abroad and for the local employees they hire there. As might be expected of arrangements with multinationals, this line of consulting is quite lucrative; consultants earn from $1,200 to $2,000 a day and research assistants $300 to $500 a day.

Moreover most of the large multinationals have their own offices for employment and salary analysis, because what they pay expatriate and indigenous employees affects their ability to hire the best people, to maintain good relations with host countries and to enhance their competitive position in the international marketplace. Since by definition multinational corporations do more than 40% of their business outside their home-base country, it is essential for them to keep abreast of the latest international economic developments, particularly in the labor markets.

Innumerable studies have been done on the labor markets in various countries, a subject that is not only economic but political dynamite given that the multinationals are frequently accused of being the exploiters of the developing and even the developed world. Books condemning the policies and motives of the multinationals abound; for many people the huge international oil conglomerates, the chemical and manufacturing trusts, the banks and other worldwide corporations are symbols of capitalism at its worst.

However one views the political role of the multinationals, their enormous impact on the world labor market is indisputable. In 1980 the multinationals employed four million people in the developing world and over 40 million in the industrialized countries. In 1977, according to a study by the International Labor Organization (ILO), approximately 20% of all manufacturing workers in Brazil were employed by multinational corporations from several different countries, and that figure had been growing since the 1960s. In Hong Kong 40% of the manufacturing laborers in the electrical and electronics industry were employed by foreign affiliates of multinationals; in Indonesia the figure for all manufacturing was 50.4%; in Kenya about 35%; and in Nigeria about 20%.

In 1977 there were 138 major multinationals in the Philippines employing 55% of the manufacturing workers there. In Singapore fully owned and joint-venture affiliates of multinationals together employed about 70% of the manufacturing workers.

The percentage of manufacturing employees hired by multinationals is generally lower in the developed countries with two notable exceptions: Canada and the United States. A 1976 ILO study revealed that in both countries multinationals employed 34% of all manufacturing workers. Next came Austria with 21%, Belgium with 13%, the United Kingdom with 8%, West Germany with 5% and France with 4%. (Given the date of the study, the figures may have changed somewhat.) However, despite their lower percentages of workers employed by multinationals, industrialized countries with large manufacturing plant, work force and industrial capacity tend to have larger total numbers of employees working for multinationals, which need highly skilled labor.

In 1972 about 80% of all executives hired by U.S. multinational firms for work overseas were Americans. Because of the cost of transferring American executives and paying their taxes while they were abroad, the figure by 1980 had shrunk to about 37%. New tax laws for Americans abroad, effective in 1982, allow the first $75,000 of income to be tax free, and the number of deductible expenses has been increased. This may result in raising the number of expatriate American managers, but it is not at all certain.

Although the practice is rare today in the world of multinationals, Japanese firms use only Japanese in top and middle-management positions in developing as well as developed nations, including the United States and Western European countries, because they feel their extraordinary success with employer-worker relations and managerial expertise have been crucial to the economic triumphs of Japanese businesses.

Japanese companies currently have over 300 plants in the United States employing about 120,000 Americans and that number is growing. They are also cooperating with firms in the United Kingdom in manufacturing autos, electronics and other products and are expanding rapidly into other developed countries as well to avoid import restrictions and have more immediate access to these markets. In the United States some union critics accuse the Japanese of paying less than union-scale wages, and some antibias suits have been brought against Japanese multinationals for, among other things, employing only male Japanese nationals in management positions. Recently some Japanese affiliates in the United States—SANYO Electric Company in California and Sharp Manufacturing Company in Tennessee—have been unionized. Affiliates constructing new plants in the United States, such as the Honda plant being built in the Midwest, are taking every precaution to avoid this challenge to their freedom of action, and a great battle looms in the United States as well as in Western Europe between Japanese companies and local unions.

The trend among multinationals of most countries, however, is toward greater employment of indigenous managerial talent, often trained in the United States or Western Europe, for middle and upper-middle positions in foreign affiliates.

One reason for this trend is the desire to internationalize the corporations and create a greater degree of self-sufficiency in the affiliates. But another reason, and probably a more important one, is the staggering costs of attracting executives to work abroad by paying them competitive and higher salaries and giving them living adjustments to maintain their life styles. The following table shows what an executive earning $50,000 a year with a wife and two children living in Washington, D.C. must be paid to compensate for separation from home and the higher living costs in the various countries indicated. Further costs to the employer associated with taxes, relocation and home leaves *are not* computed into these figures. The table simply estimates the pay necessary to attract managers to leave.

U.S. executives often receive considerably more than indigenous managers holding identical or similar jobs in a local industry in the same country. This is also true for managers of multinationals home-based in other countries, such as the United Kingdom, West Germany or Japan. The problems that constantly arise from this disparity in pay are

Table 1

SALARY COMPENSATION FOR U.S. EXECUTIVE WITH FAMILY OF FOUR LIVING IN WASHINGTON, D.C. AND EARNING $50,000

	U.S. $
Riyadh, Saudi Arabia	$128,500
Tokyo, Japan	$121,500
Hong Kong	$ 90,000
Paris, France	$ 89,500
Johannesburg, South Africa	$ 88,000
Rio de Janeiro, Brazil	$ 87,500
London, United Kingdom	$ 87,000
Singapore	$ 84,000
Bonn, West Germany	$ 79,500
Mexico City, Mexico	$ 78,000
Rome, Italy	$ 71,500
Toronto, Canada	$ 62,000

Source: Analyzed from data available from Organization Resources Counselors, New York, USA.

another reason why the number of expatriates working as managers in multinational affiliates has declined.

A second set of salary figures shows that in many countries the cost to the employer of supporting an expatriate executive is much higher than merely his salary. A manager earning $40,000 will cost his or her employer (after cost of living adjustments, housing, educational allowances, [if necessary], home leave, travel allotments, transportation, personal protection [if necessary], tax supports and other payments) $142,000 in Nigeria, $120,000 in Sweden, $112,000 in Japan, $100,000 in Switzerland, $92,000 in West Germany and downward to $46,000 in Canada.

Remembering the message of Table 1, an executive earning $50,000 in the United States will certainly demand more than that as a base salary to move to another country, as will his counterpart in the United Kingdom or any of the other industrialized nations. However, lest one feel too sorry about the high costs of staffing affiliates with expatriates, it must be remembered that virtually all of the 50 largest industrial corporations in the world, with annual sales ranging from $73 million to $3.5 billion, are multinationals. They have proven thoroughly capable of meeting their payroll challenges in the past and will most likely weather the current world-wide economic contraction.

The salaries of office and clerical employees in the many branches of multinationals also tend to be higher than those of employees of locally owned companies. This is less true in developed countries than developing ones, but there is still a difference, and even in the countries of Western Europe employment by multinationals is preferred. For example, while the average annual salary of a bilingual secretary in West Germany for all firms is 36,400 marks ($16,380), multinationals, particularly American, pay up to 48,000 marks ($21,600). In Belgium the rate is 520,000 Belgian francs ($15,600) for all firms; multinationals pay up to 565,000 Belgian francs ($16,950). In Switzerland the rate is 37,500 Swiss francs ($21,000); multinationals sometimes pay up to 40,500 Swiss francs ($22,680).

These figures, however, indicate a relatively small increase in pay, less than in some developing countries, where a bilingual secretary can earn as much as 20% to 30% more working for a multinational company rather than a national firm. For example, a bilingual secretary in Pakistan may be offered a salary of 10,000 rupees ($1,016) per year by a multinational firm, while the rate for all firms is more in the range of 7,500 rupees to 8,250 rupees ($762 to $838).

Multinationals clearly benefit from increased profits made possible by using cheaper labor to manufacture products in some developing countries; at the same time, they pay indus-trial labor higher wages (generally) than do national firms. This causes disruptions in the local labor markets and stunts indigenous industrial development, and in this sense multinationals exploit local economic growth for the benefit of more sophisticated international operations.

Studies and information collected by the International Labor Office show that multinationals pay manufacturing wages ranging from 130% to 170% higher than the wages offered by national enterprises; many of the countries where this difference is largest are in Latin America, with Brazil, Chile, Columbia, and Mexico the leading examples. In Mexico, for instance, during the past decade the multinationals paid workers in the rubber products industry about 2.7 times as much as Mexican companies paid.

A few more examples from Africa and Asia will show the differences between manufacturing salaries offered by multinationals and average wages paid by local firms. In Morocco multinationals recommend paying about 12,000 dirhams to 14,000 dirhams ($2,264 to $2,641) a year; the average Moroccan factory wage in 1979 was 7,720 dirhams ($1,457) a year. A factory worker in Bangladesh is offered from 8,000 takas to 10,000 takas ($451 to $563) a year by the multinationals; the average local wage in 1977 was 3,011 takas ($170) a year, and inflation has not been that significant. In the Philippines a factory worker employed by a multinational can make 10,000 pesos ($1,232) a year, almost twice the average annual wage—5,105 pesos ($629)—paid by Filipino firms in 1979.

Undoubtedly in these countries it is to the advantage of a local worker to find employment with an affiliate of a multinational, and in turn the latter can select the most qualified people. Multinational corporations are able to pay more for employees at all levels and in doing so exert influence on the direction of economic development in all countries of the world.

These multinational salaries cause increases in the pay

scales for workers in developing countries, and the great discrepancies between salaries in the developing and the developed worlds are lessening with time as the world economy, both products and markets, becomes more interdependent; eventually wages and costs will tend to equalize. At the same time, national governments strive to protect and foster the development of their own economies and bring the standard of living for all up to that made possible by employment with multinationals.

Even though the multinationals pay factory workers in developing countries higher than the going rate, they still pay much less than they would for the same work in developed countries. Labor unions in North America, Western Europe and some of the more advanced developing nations claim that the cheap labor which makes price advantages possible for multinationals operating abroad takes jobs from the home work force. The unions stress that multinationals or their affiliates, as in the case of the Japanese manufacturers mentioned, avoid unionization wherever they are.

Labor unions are attempting to cooperate transnationally in an effort to maintain minimum wage levels that will protect the jobs of higher paid workers in the industrialized countries. Increasing labor costs in the developing nations are viewed by some unionists as ultimately beneficial to all workers, but in the fiercely competitive and undercapitalized world economy, union cooperation is far from a reality.

Pay disparities within a country and pay disparities between countries when labor at different cost competes for the same jobs (e.g., U.S. electronics industry pay scales as opposed to electronics industry pay levels in Hong Kong) are two of the economic woes blamed on multinationals and their salary and hiring policies. Whatever the talk about exporting skills and even jobs or ultimate equalization of standards of living, a manufacturing worker in Hong Kong made about

$8.30 a day in 1980 and a manufacturing worker in the United States made about $58.16 a day, or approximately seven times as much. This difference obviously makes it cheaper to produce certain equipment in Hong Kong and unquestionably costs some jobs in the United States. Labor unions are seriously threatened by this situation and propose to do something about it, including demands for greater import restrictions and taxes and more extensive quota systems.

Resentment in the developing world against what is viewed as the economic dominance of multinational cartels also takes political forms. In several countries multinationals are a visible representation of the presence of foreign economic power.

The resentment, however, is less shared by the employees of the multinationals, who are paid higher wages and enjoy the benefits of a higher standard of living. At worst multinational corporations exacerbate wage differences, divert domestic investment, profitability and resources to the interests of their global operations. At best they pay better and bring up other wage scales; increase local productivity and improve production techniques in general; train indigenous workers; provide interchange between the managers and workers of the world; and undeniably increase the standard of living, even if selectively and inevitably for a minority.

4

EXECUTIVES AND MANAGERS

Every seasoned traveler knows that the same product made locally in different countries varies in quality and performance. The cigarettes of some nations crumble or only the paper burns when you light them, while others are firm and draw easily. Certain light bulbs last longer than others. Some toilet papers are rough, others soft; some soap bars disintegrate when immersed in water, others make plentiful suds; some trains rattle and squeak on the flattest rail bed, others slide along smoothly and quietly.

Just as products differ from country to country, so do the paychecks and other rewards of those who make them, from the top executives to the lowest workers on the industrial ladder. Those who make the best products are not necessarily paid the best. Income scales depend on so many factors, including the cost and standard of living in the different countries, the rate of taxation, the costs of production, the relationship between industry and government, the extent of social and employee benefits, attitudes about work and a host of other considerations.

Regardless of the stature of the industrial organization

and the quality of the products manufactured, in most countries the higher paid the executive or manager the more complex the remuneration. A straight salary will not suffice when it becomes so high that much or most of it can be taxed away. Western European countries have among the highest tax rates in the world. In fact, most have higher rates than those of the United States, Canada and Australia. That is why in Europe the employee who is paid by fixed salary alone can be very unhappy; he may make enough to begin with, but once the government takes its share in taxes, he finds it difficult to get by. Therefore paying taxes is something to be avoided and deplored. (This is particularly true in nationalized industries, although the extensive social benefits tend to lessen the pain.)

To circumvent the tax structure, executives are given perquisites, or fringe benefits, which include financial opportunities, deferred payments, special bonuses, personal services and other advantages that represent a substantial and not always publicly known segment of the payment package. These perks often have enormous value and come in a staggering variety, such as expense accounts, houses (with swimming pools, gyms, tennis courts, etc.), cars, planes, private club membership, low-interest loans and mortgages, full-paid vacations, clothing, family travel and education and the free services of lawyers, accountants and investment counselors. In addition, there are a number of more personalized services, including those provided by chauffeurs, pilots, gardeners, masseurs, hairdressers, chefs, governesses, maids, fencing masters, gymnastic instructors, swimming instructors, psychiatrists and many others.

Some of the perks given to executives can be illegal or at least extralegal, such as hidden investments, numbered bank accounts (to receive undeclared payments), disguised ownership of property, privileged or even collusive investment opportunities. In most cases, however, fringe benefits of this nature are limited to higher paid executives and they do not exist everywhere. They are less frequent in countries such as Sweden, the United Kingdom, Canada and the United States, where the tax regulations are rigorously applied and evasion is difficult. (This is not to say that criminal evasion is easy anywhere, but the tolerance of tax avoidance is so much greater in some countries that the practice naturally tends to be more common in them.)

Another consideration when comparing actual incomes of executives and managers is the role of underground money, or "black money." Undeclared transactions and unrecorded earnings, which for years have been a normal business practice in many nations, are becoming increasingly prevalent at all economic levels throughout the industrialized societies. The stringent application of sales taxes and value-added taxes combined with rising income tax rates have led many to seek ways of earning income without declaring it. In Italy the percentage of underground economic deals out of all business transactions is estimated at no less than 35% and in many other countries from 10% to 20%; in the United States some economists put the figure as high as 25%. Because of the effectiveness of the value-added tax in keeping track of incomes, particularly in the United Kingdom, declaring part but not all of the earnings in a transaction has become a fine art. For example, part of a construction job may be openly declared to account for the value of materials bought and used, while another part is kept secret, with an arrangement for direct and unrecorded payment to the contractor. When this is done in the case of a large housing project, for example, the evasion can be substantial.

It is noteworthy that such black money activity has grown in countries that have traditionally prided themselves on respect and obedience for the law and governmental regulations. A recent poll in Britain showed that while only 31% considered tax evasion wrong, 59% condemned fox hunting and 60% disapproved of adultery, almost twice the number of those opposed to "fiddling." Black money, moreover, is found in many professions and occupations, particularly among the self-employed.

It is impossible to place an exact monetary value on the amount that perks and black money practices add to salaries in different countries. Yet these fringes play a very important role in income compensation, particularly among executives, who have greater access to complex financial arrangements. In various Western European countries the use of company-owned cars by executives for both business and personal purposes is so significant and widespread that surveys have been made to determine which car model an executive at a given level should be entitled to. The accompanying table synopsizes one such study done by Management Center Europe (a branch of the American Management Association International) to demonstrate just how essential this benefit has become as a part of compensation policies. Obviously the higher the rank of the executive, the more expensive the car—often accompanied by a chauffeur. At the most exalted levels two cars are sometimes provided.

The number of executives receiving cars is by far the highest in Britain, where perks in general are estimated to constitute 30% to 35% of total executive remuneration. This is due to relatively low salaries and high taxes, making fringe benefits vitally important in the competition for managers. So ubiquitous is the company car in Britain that over one-half of all cars sold there annually are bought by firms. Visitors to London's West End are often awed by the vast number of gleaming automobiles surging powerfully along the streets. One could easily imagine that this is the industrial promised land, where everyone owns a machine and

Table 1

MOST POPULAR BRAND AND MODEL* OF
COMPANY CAR FOR EXECUTIVES IN FIVE COUNTRIES

	Chief Executive	% of Total Receiving Car	Top Management	% of Total Receiving Car
Belgium	BMW 525	78	Citroen CX2400	56
France	Peugeot 605	85	Peugeot 504	47
Germany, West	Mercedes 280	92	Mercedes 250	47
Switzerland	Mercedes 280	74	Mercedes 280	23
United Kingdom	Jaguar 4.2	99	Rover 3500	90

*Model of car is subject to change.
Source: Management Center Europe.

45

travels in magnificent style through the most affluent neighborhoods. Actually he is more than likely observing executive perks in motion past fashionable shops whose expensive items are very possibly purchased with expense account money.

In every country I visited, I impertinently asked executives, "Is it here in your country that the executives and managers are the highest paid in the world?" The answer would always come heatedly: "Here? In this country? Certainly not. You can see for yourself we are being destroyed by inflation and taxes. Believe me, only the workers make money in this country!"

In nearly all industries the very highest paid executives in the world are found in the United States. A few comparisons help to illustrate this point. In 1977 Giovanni Agnelli, the chairman of Fiat and a member of the family that owns the company, declared an income of 258 million lire ($206,400) from his job. In 1978 Henry Ford, also a wealthy and powerful man whose grandfather founded the company bearing his name, declared an income of $1,056,000 from his position as chairman of the Ford Motor Company. Although Ford is larger than Fiat, they are both among the world's very biggest corporations. Yet the difference between the two salaries is enormous.

In another instance Sir David Steel declared an income in 1979 of £120,385 ($232,000) as chairman of the British Petroleum Company Ltd., which is one of the 15 largest corporations in the world. In 1980 Robert O. Anderson, chairman of Atlantic Richfield Company, an oil company of approximately the same size as British Petroleum, declared total compensation of $1,650,000.

These two comparisons, of course, are not conclusive. There are perks and other forms of income not taken into account in the figures. Also, there are certainly cases of non-Americans earning more than Americans who have positions of similar importance and responsibility in the United States. For example, in 1979 the chairman of Taisho Seiyaku Company, a Japanese pharmaceutical firm, was reportedly paid 2 billion yen ($9.2 million), a staggering figure for any executive.

Nevertheless in 1980 there were 23 American chief executives who each earned more than $1.5 million in total remuneration, a figure equaled in no other country. In the same year the highest paid Western European executives rarely earned more than $800,000, and that level of salary was very unusual indeed.

Not only are the top American executives the best paid in the world, their salaries are also the most publicized. One reason for this disclosure is that the U.S. Securities and Exchange Commission, a federal regulatory agency, requires publication of the salaries of the top executives in publicly held corporations as protection for the stockholders. There are no similar regulations requiring publication of the salaries of company executives elsewhere, and when incomes are public information in other countries, such as Sweden, they are listed by individual, not by position.

Another reason for the publicity is the American fascination with monetary proof of success. The incomes of not only executives but also of athletes, entertainers, lawyers, criminals and others are constantly in the news. Furthermore the race for salaries begins early in a career, and the starting salaries of recent graduates of leading law schools (up to $48,000 per year) and business schools (up to $40,000 a year) are the subject of endless newspaper and magazine articles.

Wealth creates class in the United States and thus income provides a yardstick of social position. In more traditional societies, where class has already been created over centu-

47

ries by an interplay of power, lineage and wealth, public awareness of immense incomes would only serve to fan resentments that are often close to the surface. Thus, in the United Kingdom executives positively enjoy demonstrating how little they make in comparison with their counterparts in most other industrialized countries, and the same is claimed, although with less justification, in France, Switzerland, Belgium and other European countries.

In the United States the huge salaries paid at the top levels in large corporations emphasize short-term gains by stressing immediate individual rewards at the expense of loyalty to a company and its long-term interests. Changing jobs is more common in America than in Europe; in fact, in some industries an individual executive must jump from one company to another in order to maximize his or her salary. This preoccupation with quick, individual rewards creates a more volatile atmosphere than exists in most European countries and is the very antithesis of the system in Japan.

Studies of leading corporations in the United States indicate the extreme degree of individual opportunism among American executives. About 50% of college recruits leave their first company before the end of five years, and only 23% of senior American managers interviewed said that they believed corporate loyalty is important for success. Yet the study also found that American corporations pay their top people high salaries and offer maximum recognition in the hopes of obtaining their loyalty as much as for any other motive.

In Japan there is a collective, intermingling approach toward business and social activity, and lifelong loyalty to a firm is the normal pattern of a career. Job changers are called "butterflies" and rarely succeed, being considered undependable and prone to placing individual welfare before that of the group. In the current awe over Japanese managerial success the themes of collective action and loyalty to a firm are singled out as prime explanations for the greater long-term innovation and productivity that characterizes Japanese industry. Nothing is more alien to the Japanese than the spectacle of managers in the United States garnering salary increases at the same time their corporations' profits are declining or actually losing money, as has been true in numerous cases in the past few years.

At least one-third of total annual remuneration in Japan comes in the form of bonuses based on profitability; both executive and worker salaries rise or fall in accordance with the changing conditions and performance of a company. Bonuses tied to performance for chief and senior executives are universal in Japan and are becoming more widespread in the United States, as the rigors of economic competition have grown and demands for greater productivity are stimulating reforms. Similar merit bonuses are given to over one-half of the executives in Britain, but while growing in number, they are less frequent on the Continent.

The following table shows the salary ranges of chief executives in 11 countries. The data presented, with some modifications, are drawn from studies done by the Executive Compensation Service of the American Management Association. Additional studies have also been used in reaching conclusions about the data.

The table shows that while the average salaries of chief executives in Belgium, France, West Germany and Spain are consistently lower than the average in the United States, they do approximate U.S. salaries. In Brazil, Canada, Italy, Mexico and the United Kingdom the executive salaries are definitely lower. Only in Switzerland are the average salaries of chief executives for very large companies higher than those of their American counterparts. The chief executive of the Deutsche Bank in West Germany earned 796,000 marks

Table 2

TOTAL AVERAGE ANNUAL REMUNERATION FOR
CHIEF EXECUTIVES IN 12 COUNTRIES (1980)

	Companies Up to $1 Billion in Sales		Companies Over $1 Billion in Sales	
	Local Currency	U.S. $ Equivalent*	Local Currency	U.S. $ Equivalent*
Belgium				
Gross:	BF 4,851,000	$145,500	BF 9,235,000	$277,000
Net:	BF 1,891,000	$ 56,700	BF 2,864,000	$ 85,900
Brazil				
Gross:	Cr 4,000,000	$ 32,000	Cr 6,920,000	$ 55,400
Net:	NA	NA	NA	NA
Canada				
Gross:	C$ 116,500	$ 97,900	NA	NA
Net:	NA	NA	NA	NA
France				
Gross:	FF 1,200,000	$216,000	NA	NA
Net:	FF 623,800	$112,100	NA	NA
Germany, West				
Gross:	DM 504,600	$227,000	DM 690,000	$310,500
Net:	DM 227,000	$102,100	NA	NA

	Local Currency	U.S. $ Equivalent*	Local Currency	U.S. $ Equivalent*
Italy				
Gross:	Lira 126,360,000	$101,100	NA	NA
Net:	Lira 73,320,000	$ 58,650	NA	NA
Mexico				
Gross:	Peso 1,896,000	$ 75,800	Peso 2,304,000	$ 92,200
Net:	NA	NA	NA	NA
Netherlands				
Gross:	DFL 288,100	$118,100	DFL 321,750	$131,900
Net:	DFL 132,200	$ 54,200	DFL 126,000	$ 51,600
Spain				
Gross:	Pta 16,116,100	$161,200	NA	NA
Net:	Pta 8,229,000	$ 82,300	NA	NA
Switzerland				
Gross:	SF 317,400	$177,700	SF 740,200	$414,500
Net:	SF 187,300	$104,900	SF 427,000	$239,100
United Kingdom				
Gross:	£ 60,700	$117,200	£ 69,000	$133,200
Net:	£ 30,190	$ 58,300	£ 33,030	$ 63,700
United States				
Gross:	$ 311,000	—	$ 402,000	—
Net:	$ 173,000	—	$ 200,000	—

*1982.

($358,200) in 1980. Chief executives of other large banks and companies the size of Volkswagenwerk, Daimler-Benz and BMW are paid in the $400,000 to $500,000 range; in the United States in 1980 there were 70 chief executives whose remuneration equaled $1 million or more.

Of course there are individual corporate executives throughout Europe, Latin America, Japan, Canada, Australia and the Middle East who receive more money than American executives, but they are surprisingly rare and frequently they are individual entrepreneurs, such as Rupert Murdoch of Australia, oil sheiks or political rulers. President Sese Mobutu of Zaire, whose income is reportedly staggering, is a well-publicized example of the last type of "executive." But the fact remains that the average American chief executive is the best paid in the world, just as 11 of the 15 largest corporations in the world and approximately 50 of the largest 150 are American.

Understandably U.S. chief executives in the very largest corporations earn more, but Americans also get higher pay on the average for jobs with similar or even less responsibility and scope than their international counterparts. A good illustration, and one of many, is a comparison of the remuneration of the chief executive officers of two huge manufacturers of electrical equipment: the Westinghouse Corporation in the United States and the Matsushita Electric Industrial Company in Japan. In 1980 the American company employed 145,000 people and had a net income of $402.9 million from sales of $8.5 billion in 1980; its chairman earned $673,000. The Japanese company employed 107,000 people and had a net income of $543 million from sales of $12.7 billion; its president earned slightly less than half as much, $333,000. Although fringe benefits and perks not considered here might increase the amount of the Japanese executive's income relative to that of the American, the cash difference is still very striking. (The CEO of McGraw-Edison, a smaller American electrical company with 35,000 employees and a net income of $51 million on sales of $2.26 billion in 1980, earned $856,000 in total remuneration!)

Whether you think chief executives around the world and Americans in particular are overpaid depends on your politics, your own income and your attitude toward the purpose and value of work. Some corporate leaders are famous for their lavish life styles. Certain American oil executives and pharmaceutical magnates, to name two lucrative industrial areas, are renowned for the luxuries and possessions they have garnered through their jobs. Other executives maintain a low profile, especially in countries where wealth is resented or executives are in danger of being kidnapped or the victims of other acts of violence.

Attitudes about the incomes and living habits of top executives differ from country to country. In Britain some of the really demanding executive jobs are held by Americans and other foreigners. One of the most famous examples is Ian MacGregor, an American citizen who was born in Scotland. In 1980 MacGregor, who was a partner at Lazard Freres and Company, was appointed chairman of the British Steel Corporation for three years at a salary of £48,500 ($93,600). In addition the British government paid a "transfer fee" of $1.6 million to Lazard Freres as compensation for the use of his services. Another example is Sir Michael Edwardes, the South African chairman of BL Ltd. (formerly British Leyland), the huge nationalized automobile company. Several people in Britain remarked of this situation and the world of top executives in general: "Since the Americans and similar types work all the time they make more money. Good luck to them. But I wouldn't be one of them for anything." This was not always an expression of resentment as much as a reflection of a genuine feeling that the sacrifices and obsessive dedication required for executive success were not always worth the monetary rewards.

Another reaction expressed in Britain, and shared in many countries on the continent and in Japan, was amazement at the degree of continual insecurity that American business-men feel about their jobs, their futures and their basic wel-fare. The atmosphere of unbridled competition, the irrational dismissals and the constant tension over possible job termi-nation, and the seeming need to change companies repeat-edly bemuse many people in Europe and Japan, who value continuity and some sense of security from frequent, dis-turbing tension and change.

This is not to say that competition is any less keen in France, West Germany, Switzerland or Japan. However, the view in those countries is that Americans often exhaust themselves in a frantic atmosphere of suspicion and rivalry, and the enormous financial rewards of executive success reflect the uncertainty of power and position and the need for immediate, palpable gratification. Power in those na-tions can be more extensive and arbitrary, not to say auto-cratic, and much more concentrated in the hands of selec-tive, self-perpetuating elites. These elites often wish to avoid unnecessary identification and consider publicity about cash salaries embarrassing and even dangerous. They view such fringe benefits as housing and transportation as assurances of privacy and protection.

The attitude of the Japanese toward individual success is very different from that found in America. Japan's spectac-ular commercial achievements in the international market in recent years have been a source of envy and often the cause of disgruntlement in the rest of the world. Top executive salaries in Japan rarely exceed $350,000 to $450,000, but Japanese executives also benefit from free or company-financed housing, cars and very inclusive expense accounts.

Remuneration has always been tied to a firm's profitability, however, and since the entire career of a Japanese executive is almost always inextricably bound to one company, from the first job to retirement, compensation levels have tended to rise with the growth of Japanese companies. Long-term growth is to the advantage of everyone—executives and workers as well as banks and other financial institutions and the government, all of which are involved in the planning and investment of the corporations.

In Japan the selection process for the first job is very competitive, beginning in the formative years with social training and education. The largest corporations take the best candidates from the prestigious universities and schools and pay the largest remuneration over the years. The most desirable applicants come from the University of Tokyo; almost all key jobs in business, government and many of the professions are held by graduates of the university. Although entrance exams are open and based on merit, in reality over two-thirds of the students come from the higher social and economic strata, because the cost of intense and lengthy preparations for passing the rigorous entrance exams favors the children of wealthier families. This process helps to perpetuate the closely knit elite in government and business that monopolizes control of all important decision-making processes in Japan. Unlike in the United States and some other countries, top executives rarely "begin at the bottom."

A young Japanese university graduate entering a business starts work in a section, earning about $15,000 to $20,000 in the beginning and eventually rising to $40,000 or more when he becomes a section chief *(kaho)* sometime in his late thirties or early forties. At this stage his expense account can equal about one-half of his salary. The next major promotion is to department chief *(busho)*, occurring around the age of 45 to 50, when the salary becomes $60,000 to $100,000 plus an expense account and housing benefits that amount to about three quarters of the salary. The next level is the job of director, which pays as much as $200,000 a year, with benefits and an expense account that often equal the total salary.

The tradition of business entertainment is probably more important in Japan than in any other industrial country. Executive socializing serves not only to solicit business, but also to deal with problems within a company and to maintain harmonious relations between employers and employees. Therefore a very wide range of off-the-job activities are justified as company expenses. Since much of a Japanese executive's life revolves around his work, a very large part of his expenses, including dinners several times a week, gifts, seats at entertainment events and trips, is considered business related. The higher up the executive ladder he goes, the more of his activities outside the office are paid for as necessary company entertainment.

The job of chief executive in firms of all sizes carries great social prestige. Because of the stable levels of management below, there is less relentless operational pressure on Japanese CEOs than on their counterparts in the United States and Western Europe. Furthermore those competent, loyal, hard-working Japanese who are qualified but not chosen to become top executives are assured of keeping their jobs, unlike in the United States, where those who lose out in the competition for the top position in a company generally find it difficult to remain there. Even if Japanese executives are not particularly competent, suitable work is still found for them either in their own firm or an associated company.

The elitist selection process for executives also exists in Western Europe, but to a less rigorous extent. Certain educational backgrounds and appropriate social standing ease the path to high positions. In France the Ecole Nationale d'Administration plays a role somewhat similar to that of the University of Tokyo for people entering government and business, and a few other prestigious universities and technical schools in France and other European countries serve essentially the same selecting function.

Some business schools in the United States, such as Harvard, Chicago and Stanford, carry considerable weight in the selection of recent graduates by corporations, but at least for the present, the job selection process has less of the elitist overtones found in other countries. Whether this will remain true remains to be seen. The key to such a development historically would seem to be a closer connection between government and business leaders drawn from the same social and educational class, something that characterizes the more traditional societies but is less evident in the United States, Canada and Australia.

Partly because of the homogeneity of young additions to the executive ranks and partly because the steps up the ladder are more predictable, the earnings increments of managers in Japan and Western Europe are more evenly balanced throughout their careers than those of American executives. Middle- and upper-level executives in these countries are generally better paid than their counterparts in the United States and the increase in responsibility and remuneration follows a more continuous and dependable path.

Table 3 compares (in U.S. dollars) executive salaries at three levels—lower-middle, middle and upper-middle—in the United States with salaries for equivalent positions in 12 other countries. The ratio of U.S. salaries to those in other countries generally remains the same as the salaries move toward upper management. Only in top executive positions (see Table 2) do executive salaries in the United States surpass, on the average, those in Belgium, France, West Germany and the Netherlands. However, U.S. executives at all

Table 3

THREE MID-RANGE EXECUTIVE SALARY LEVELS IN 13 COUNTRIES, IN U.S. DOLLARS (1981)

	LOWER-MIDDLE		MIDDLE		UPPER-MIDDLE	
	($) Gross	($) Net	($) Gross	($) Net	($) Gross	($) Net
U.S.	**45,356**	**29,242**	**64,096**	**37,916**	**86,754**	**47,720**
Australia	31,890	22,172	46,177	25,566	60,050	33,971
Belgium	63,866	38,293	96,315	50,697	131,231	62,162
Canada	38,560	26,537	52,192	33,240	77,583	44,813
France	54,048	40,811	75,168	55,382	108,871	75,362
Germany, West	62,514	40,653	91,381	54,809	125,076	70,163
Netherlands	56,470	31,420	83,352	40,080	112,422	48,599
Singapore	34,850	24,794	58,698	39,868	91,680	59,657
South Africa	32,085	25,707	44,951	33,076	60,819	41,133
Spain	39,413	30,898	58,018	43,762	84,258	59,800
Sweden	40,954	17,657	55,846	19,746	73,165	21,551
Switzerland	71,831	52,093	100,390	67,132	139,661	87,538
United Kingdom	25,875	19,218	36,650	25,565	49,220	32,738

Source: Employment Conditions Abroad Ltd., 16 Devonshire Street, London W1, U.K.

levels earn more than their counterparts in Australia, Canada, South Africa, Spain, Sweden and the United Kingdom.

Table 4, which is in pounds, compares three mid-range executive salary levels in the United Kingdom with those for equivalent jobs in 16 other countries. The United Kingdom is very low paying in comparison with most of the other countries, and as in Table 3, the United States trails Belgium, France, West Germany and Switzerland in these middle executive pay levels.

To give life to these two tables, I will compare the earning situation of a French executive with that of an English executive. The Frenchman, who is managing director of a textile firm in Lille, earns £36,000 ($69,480) a year, with an annual bonus of £6,000 ($11,580) and a small percentage commission on the company's profits; the firm employs about 100 people and has annual sales of £10 million ($19.3 million). The Englishman earns £21,000 ($40,530) a year in total for his job as joint managing director of a manufacturing firm near Bolton, which employs over 400 people and has annual sales of £16 million ($30.88 million). Both men have company cars—a Ford Granada Ghia for the English executive, a Mercedes Benz for the French executive— and expense accounts, of which the Frenchman's is more extensive. The Englishman lives in his own house and pays the mortgage; the French executive lives in a company house, which he has the option to buy at any time he chooses. The two companies are similar in size and the two jobs have comparable responsibilities.

Clearly the Frenchman is better remunerated through pay and benefits than his English colleague and at more or less the same ratio as indicated in Table 3. The comparison provides a striking example of the variance in executive rewards in two countries just a small body of water apart from each other. However, the Frenchman gets one final perk that

Table 4

THREE MID-RANGE EXECUTIVE SALARY LEVELS IN 17 COUNTRIES, IN BRITISH POUNDS (1981)

	LOWER-MIDDLE		MIDDLE		UPPER-MIDDLE	
	(£) Gross	(£) Net	(£) Gross	(£) Net	(£) Gross	(£) Net
United Kingdom	**13,100**	**9,500**	**17,500**	**12,050**	**23,950**	**15,350**
Australia	17,000	11,800	23,950	14,800	31,400	17,750
Belgium	24,600	14,600	35,400	18,700	50,900	23,750
Canada	17,250	13,150	23,400	16,500	33,300	21,250
Denmark	18,300	8,500	25,500	10,700	35,150	13,650
France	22,500	17,500	31,550	23,550	45,050	32,000
Germany, West	23,400	16,400	33,400	21,400	52,200	29,950
Greece	13,150	8,350	19,050	10,950	NA	NA
Ireland	11,750	8,400	15,600	10,350	20,950	12,550
Italy	14,700	10,150	21,050	14,250	30,050	19,250
Netherlands	19,550	11,500	27,900	14,350	38,000	17,450
Singapore	17,800	13,150	27,750	19,800	43,550	30,100
South Africa	15,850	12,350	22,100	15,750	30,900	20,150
Spain	16,600	12,050	24,400	18,200	32,600	23,250
Sweden	18,050	8,150	23,600	9,050	30,600	10,100
Switzerland	27,700	19,350	39,000	25,050	53,150	32,000
United States	21,650	13,500	29,200	16,900	40,350	21,700

Source: Employment Conditions Abroad Ltd., 16 Devonshire St., London W1, England, U.K.

is not shared—or particularly desired—by the English director: *the firm in Lille provides a full-time bodyguard for him.*

The final table compares representative salaries for four key upper management positions in 10 countries, giving the salaries in local currency and the equivalent in U.S. dollars and British pounds. The figures show that upper management positions are also generally better paid in half the countries listed than they are in the United Kingdom and the United States. It must be pointed out that there is no direct monetary measure of the perks and benefits that accrue to jobs in the various countries.

Table 5 is drawn principally from the studies of the American Management Association, its related Management Center in Europe and Management Center in Canada and its *International Compensation Reports.*

Managers in Communist countries make considerably less than their counterparts in the capitalist world, but since wages and prices are fixed by the government, the actual monetary amount of pay is less important than the benefits that go with jobs at various levels. In Poland and Hungary there has been a greater degree of economic flexibility than in the rest of the Eastern European countries, although the turmoil in Poland has made any analysis of the economic situation there extremely difficult.

In 1979 a middle manager of a factory in Poland, or similar type of production unit, of intermediate size could earn from 12,000 to 18,000 zlotys a month ($150 to $225) and also expect a bonus of between 10,000 to 20,000 zlotys ($125 to $250) every three months. This would mean an annual total salary of approximately 174,000 to 276,000 zlotys ($2,175 to $3,450). A higher level manager could receive about 360,000 zlotys ($4,500), and of course, some managers and entrepreneurs may earn far more.

For managers in Communist nations the car is a tradi-

Table 5
TOTAL GROSS ANNUAL REMUNERATION* FOR FOUR UPPER MANAGEMENT POSITIONS IN 10 COUNTRIES (1980)

	DIRECTOR OF SALES			DIRECTOR OF ENGINEERING			DIRECTOR OF FINANCE			DIRECTOR OF RESEARCH		
	Local Currency	U.S. $	British £	Local Currency	U.S. $	British £	Local Currency	U.S. $	British £	Local Currency	U.S. $	British £
Belgium	BF 6,160,000	$198,100	£103,012	BF 3,487,000	$112,100	£58,292	BF 4,362,000	$140,300	£72,956	BF 4,026,000	$129,500	£67,340
Canada	C$ 49,500	$59,400	£30,888	C$ 55,000	$66,000	£34,320	C$ 57,000	$68,400	£35,568	C$ 41,800	$50,160	£26,083
France	FF 701,400	$157,000	£81,640	FF 701,400	$157,000	£81,640	FF 664,900	$148,800	£77,376	FF 598,900	$127,300	£66,196
Germany, West	DM 306,700	$158,900	£82,628	DM 201,100	$104,100	£54,132	DM 306,700	$158,900	£82,628	DM 250,000	$129,500	£67,340
Italy	Lira 69,700,000	$75,900	£39,468	Lira 66,550,000	$72,400	£37,648	Lira 79,200,000	$86,200	£44,824	Lira 65,080,000	$70,000	£36,400
Netherlands	DFL 271,300	$129,200	£67,184	DFL 197,200	$93,900	£48,828	DFL 245,100	$116,700	£60,684	DFL 212,700	$101,300	£52,676
Spain	Pta 8,693,000	$110,700	£57,564	Pta 8,402,000	$107,000	£55,640	Pta 13,109,000	$167,000	£86,840	Pta 6,430,000	$81,900	£42,588
Switzerland	SF 269,200	$153,900	£80,028	SF 186,000	$106,400	£55,328	SF 338,800	$193,100	£100,412	SF 273,500	$156,400	£81,328
United Kingdom	£ 43,310	$105,200		£ 32,280	$78,400		£ 43,790	$106,300		£ 40,170	$97,500	
United States	$ 119,000		£61,880	$ 101,800		£52,936	$ 153,100		£76,612	$ 111,800		£58,136

*Paid by companies with $500 million (£260 million) to $1 billion (£520 million) in sales.
Source: American Management Association Executive Compensation Service.

tional perk, with maintenance and gas allowances that are transferable or even salable in some cases. Another perk that has become highly prized among executives, labor leaders and party officials in Poland is a passport stamped to permit importation of goods without the obligation of paying duties, making a trip to the West a lucrative opportunity. Special educational programs are sometimes made available for the children of managers and party bureaucrats; until recently the minister of education could grant, at his discretion, about one-quarter of all state university entry positions to children of party members and managers.

In the Soviet Union, such perks as special housing, made famous in the West by the publicity about "little dachas" in the woods for the chosen few, free vacations to selected resorts on the Black Sea and better and more food are among the noncash emoluments of the managerial class. Also, the automobile is viewed as indispensable for those with higher responsibilities.

Since managerial position in the Communist world is so closely connected with political power, it is virtually impossible to separate the two when discussing incomes. In addition the rigid centralization of the economy in the USSR and most of the Soviet-bloc countries often permits only comparisons of specific jobs rather than general salary levels, for there is no free-market apparatus to encourage competition for executive incomes.

If economic decentralization continues in such nations as Poland, Hungary, Czechoslovakia and perhaps China, it will become easier to discuss managers by level of responsibility and experience apart from their specific managerial or political functions, as is so often the case now. For the time being, it remains very difficult to compare the compensation of managers in the Communist nations with that of their counterparts in the West and non-Communist Asia.

In the capitalist world, when a method proves superior in the marketplace at a given time, the tendency is for others to imitate it or borrow from it. However, the success story of the moment, Japan, is based upon a unique social and cultural heritage that perhaps defies imitation. Moreover Western nations do not necessarily wish to imitate much of what they find in Japan. Yet, as industrialization becomes more widespread, international compensation practices, including those found in Japan, will trend toward a common level throughout the world, as they have already in the industries dominated by multinational corporations.

5

EDUCATION, LAW AND MEDICINE

Comparing the salaries of the three major professions in countries around the world presents special challenges in each case. All three are intrigued by the incomes of those in their own group, but their attitudes toward disclosing their earnings are very different.

• Teachers make lists of how much they earn and how much they really should be earning if they were properly paid.

• Lawyers usually make more money than they are willing to admit, particularly on their tax statements. The most notable exception to this lack of candor is found in the United States, where the incomes of lawyers obsess both them and those who pay for their services.

• Doctors, like lawyers, are amazingly secretive about how much they earn, and the general suspicion in which they are held in most parts of the world is due to the belief that they make staggering and often undisclosed sums of money for treating people's illnesses. Frequently such suspicions are well founded. Dentists, cast in the role of villains from one end of the globe to the other, are presumed to accrue fortunes for inflicting pain on helpless people. Both groups will go to great lengths to keep the tax authorities and their patients from finding out what they actually make.

Primary and secondary grade school teachers are the backbone of every country's educational system, and their pay indicates the importance that their society places on education. In the developing world teachers' salaries account for a larger percentage of the total expenditure for education, over 90% in most cases. In the developed world about 60% of educational funds go for salaries, allowing more to be spent on increasing physical plants and expanding curricula.

Table 1 shows the upper average salary in major cities of 29 countries for a public school teacher with a teaching diploma or graduate degree and 10 years of experience; special allowances and benefits are included in each annual figure. The salaries, which are all in U.S. dollars, are based on studies done by the International Labor Office in 1975-77 and by the Union de Banques Suisse in 1979-80. The figures have been updated to 1981 wherever possible, but there is an error factor of ($\pm$)10% because of inflation and fluctuations in the value of the various foreign currencies and the dollar. Finally, when possible, the salary of a teacher and that of a manufacturing worker in the same country are compared on a percentage basis.

With a few exceptions the salaries of secondary school teachers at the upper end of the scale are higher than those of manufacturing workers. In many developed countries the salary of a teacher on the lowest rung, a beginning teacher, is about the same or slightly less than the average annual manufacturing wage. For example, in Canada the lowest pay for a teacher is about 70% of the average manufacturing wage, in the United Kingdom 75%, in Australia about 80%, in the United States about 90% and in New Zealand 93%.

Yet in seven other highly developed countries the lowest

salary for a starting teacher is the same or slightly higher than the average annual manufacturing wage. In France the two are virtually equal and in the Netherlands almost equal; the minimum salary for a teacher is 6% higher than the average manufacturing wage in Belgium, 14% higher in West Germany, 21% higher in Sweden, 25% higher in Switzerland and 30% higher in Denmark. However, in Japan the lowest salaried teacher made only 57% of the average annual manufacturing wage in 1978-79.

In a few developing countries that were once part of the British Empire the salary of a beginning teacher is the same as or lower than the average annual manufacturing wage. In Sri Lanka the two are just about equal, while in Kenya a starting teacher's salary is about 72% of the average annual manufacturing wage, in Zambia 66% and in India about 60%. On the other hand, in countries that were once under French rule the salary for a beginning teacher is higher than the average wage for a manufacturing worker: in Mali (a former French colony) 12% higher and in Syria (a former French protectorate) about 35% higher. These and other comparisons based on available data indicate that teaching is a better paid and more prestigious profession, at least at the lower levels, in countries with previous exposure to French culture.

In most countries higher education is almost entirely under the direction of the central or, in some cases, the regional government. Professors in these countries are civil servants and their institutions are administered by the government. In several developed countries even religious educational institutions and specialized polytechnic schools are financed by the government.

In the major countries where private institutions play a significant role in higher education, such as the United States, the salary levels for professors at these institutions

Table 1

UPPER GROSS ANNUAL SALARY OF PUBLIC SECONDARY SCHOOL TEACHERS, IN U.S. DOLLARS (1982)

	Teacher's Salary in U.S. Dollars	% of Average Manufacturing Wage
Abu Dhabi	$11,197*	NA
Buenos Aires, Argentina	$ 3,850	NA
Sydney, Australia	$18,862	180
Vienna, Austria	$12,875	136
Brussels, Belgium	$18,562	133
Rio de Janeiro, Brazil	$ 4,850	153
Montreal, Canada	$19,760	133
Bogota, Colombia	$ 2,995	72
Copenhagen, Denmark	$21,856	138
Helsinki, Finland	$13,175	153
Paris, France	$16,450	137
Duesseldorf, West Germany	$22,395	151
Athens, Greece	$ 7,425	145

Hong Kong	$ 7,785	228
Dublin, Ireland	$12,215	161
Tel-Aviv, Israel	$ 5,330	NA
Milan, Italy	$ 8,800	115
Tokyo, Japan	$20,050	128
Amsterdam, the Netherlands	$21,720	126
Panama City, Panama	$ 3,295	NA
Singapore	$ 5,778	178
Johannesburg, South Africa	$ 9,101**	101
Stockholm, Sweden	$19,820	121
Geneva, Switzerland	$36,526	204
Bangkok, Thailand	$ 1,976	NA
Istanbul, Turkey	$ 2,995	360
London, United Kingdom	$13,530	124
Chicago, United States	$22,455	138
Caracas, Venezuela	$ 6,766	129

*Includes free housing.
**Whites only.
Sources: International Labor Office, *Teachers' Pay*; Union de Banques Suisse *1978 Prix et Salaries dans le Monde*, ed. 1979-80; and interviews, articles and reports.

are increasingly becoming equal, although Harvard, Yale, Princeton, California Institute of Technology, Massachusetts Institute of Technology and a few others continue to pay higher. The average salary for a full professor at these institutions is from $43,000 to $49,000 in disciplines other than law, medicine and the natural sciences, and such professors can easily earn an additional $10,000 to $15,000 a year by working summer jobs, writing, lecturing and consulting. The same salary range is paid at prestigious public universities in the United States, including the University of California at Berkeley, Wisconsin University and Rutgers University.

The salaries at both private and public law schools and medical schools are considerably higher. At the medical schools of Harvard, Yale and Michigan teaching salaries range from $60,000 to $70,000 a year and additional money from consulting and outside practice can easily increase the total remuneration to $90,000 a year and more. The salaries and outside income of teachers at law schools, both public and private, amount to slightly less than the possible earnings at medical schools, but they are generally far higher than the potential incomes for teachers in the humanities or social sciences.

In most European countries professors make the equivalent of what their counterparts in the United States earn. For example, in the United Kingdom professors can make £18,480 ($35,700) a year, and at certain institutions, such as Cambridge, Oxford and some others, an additional stipend of as much as £2,000 to £2,500 ($3,800 to $4,800) is paid to the holders of special chairs or appointments. In Belgium a full professor with 15 years of teaching experience can earn 940,000 Belgium francs ($28,200) a year plus full civil service benefits. In West Germany a high annual salary for a professor ranges from 84,000 marks to 93,000 marks

($37,800 to $41,850), based on a 13-month year. (The starting salary range for an untenured university teacher in West
Germany is less than half as much: about 35,000 marks to
40,000 marks [$15,750 to $18,000] a year.) However, many
academics in West Germany are paid for 14 months and
also receive the same generous benefits and allowances as
other civil service employees.

In most European countries professors, like authors, regularly supplement their incomes by working a variety of
jobs—consulting, representing companies or the government,
writing in their field—and simply holding more than one
academic post at the same time. In Italy some famous professors teach at two or three different institutions hundreds
of miles apart. For example, a professor might teach at the
University of Rome, at Bologna and at Florence on different
days. At the same time, he might write books, give guest
lectures, do consulting work and appear on TV.

In the developing countries professors receive low salaries, generally only slightly higher than the pay of the advanced secondary school teachers shown in Table 1. In such
countries as India, Nigeria, the Philippines, Indonesia, Argentina, Brazil, Mexico and others where higher education is
widespread and there is an enormous number of students,
professors maintain several academic posts and/or other jobs
to increase their incomes. The professor-entrepreneur is a
well known figure in these countries, even more so than in
Europe. In both the developing world and Europe the income
situation of professors is indicative of the fact that a career
in education is prestigious and can lead to many related but
relatively low paying jobs.

In Japan leading professors can earn 12 million to 14
million yen ($55,200 to $64,400) a year, and the teaching
profession, while not as prestigious as government service,
journalism or corporate business, still carries more prestige

than the legal or medical profession. Furthermore in Japan, the countries of Western Europe and other such developed nations as Australia, Canada, and the United States, there is a large and ever increasing interchange of faculty and students at all levels in many fields. This continuous intermingling tends to raise the salary expectations of the various nationalities and to force governments and private institutions to make an attempt at meeting these expectations. Although true equality in teachers' and professors' pay is impossible due to the inequalities of national wealth, education is one field where a general alignment of incomes is always taking place.

In Communist countries, although interchange with other nations is limited, education enjoys enormous prestige within national boundaries. In China full professors are paid the same 350 yuan ($196) a month, or 4,200 yuan ($2,352) a year, that vice ministers earn. They also receive handsome benefits in the form of housing, educational and travel allowances and other amenities that offset their low official salaries and express their real status. Assistant professors can earn up to 170 yuan ($97) a month, or 2,040 yuan ($1,164) a year, and beginning instructors make about the same as skilled manual workers: 50 yuan to 70 yuan ($29 to $40) a month, or 600 yuan to 840 yuan ($342 to $480) a year. In a nation where everyone earns a low income, Chinese professors do proportionately a bit better than their counterparts in the West in terms of cash and certainly much better in terms of benefits. The status of a professor in China is truly unique, because his income, when compared to salaries for professors in the developed nations, is so low while his social standing is so high.

In the Soviet Union the basic salary for a full professor has remained largely unchanged from 1960 to the present. According to studies done by economist Janet Chapman, the monthly salary of a professor in 1960 was 450 rubles ($333) and that of an assistant professor was 175 rubles ($130), amounting to an annual base salary of 5,400 rubles ($3,996) for a full professor and 2,100 rubles ($1,554) for an assistant professor; in 1975 the figures were the same. The latter salary is slightly more than the average annual manufacturing wage—1,930 rubles ($1,428)—in 1975 and about the same as the average annual manufacturing wage— 2,091 rubles ($1,547)—in 1979.

The basic salary for a professor in the Soviet Union is supplemented with increments for being a member of an academy of science, publishing books and articles, giving lectures and making public appearances. Also housing accommodations, cars and other transportation benefits are made available either free or at a cheaper price.

Far more remunerative, and often far more controversial, than education is the legal profession. Differences in the way law is practiced and the attitudes toward it are so great from country to country that in many cases it hardly seems to be the same profession. This is best demonstrated by a comparison of the legal profession in the United States and Japan, two competitive economic giants. In both countries there is a steady stream of books and articles about the problems of communicating with each other, in some cases the need for imitating one another and in others the necessity of emerging victorious, particularly in the field of foreign trade. These studies point out the vast differences in the value systems of the two countries, including the attitude toward various jobs and professions as well as work itself.

The law provides a dramatic illustration of this divergence in attitude. In the United States the profession has reached its high point in all of human history. There are now well over 500,000 lawyers in the United States, one lawyer for about 430 citizens—a higher ratio than that of doctors per capita—and the number is bounding upward with the addition of 35,000 new attorneys a year. Referring to the prodigious growth of litigation, Chief Justice Warren Burger in 1982 noted the "avalanche" of lawsuits and said: "For thirty years or more Americans have increasingly turned to the courts for relief from a range of personal stresses and anxieties. . . . The courts have been expected to fill the void created by the decline of the church, family and neighborhood unity."

The incomes of lawyers in the United States are also the wonder of the civilized world. Although the average for lawyers in all countries is still less than $45,000 a year, young graduates from the best law schools—Harvard, Columbia, Stanford, Yale, Chicago, the University of California at Berkeley—now start at $38,000 to $46,000 a year. They plan to be making about $90,000 a year when they are taken on as a partner in a firm. At the big law firms they can anticipate making over $200,000 a year three or four years after becoming a partner and then the sky is the only limit for the very fortunate and/or gifted. Earnings of $500,000 to $1 million a year are perfectly possible, and a lawyer who handles liability suits can make millions of dollars for himself on just a few cases.

Lawyers are admired, feared, envied, resented, and often hated because of their skill, influence and power. In a few years, when there will probably be too many members of the various bars, circumstances may change, but in the meantime law is the most appealing and impressive, if not the most prestigious, profession in the United States.

Moreover, the practice of international law has become increasingly Americanized, as American lawyers fan out around the world in concert with American businessmen, drawing up contracts, litigating on behalf of and against native enterprises and governments. Corporate lawyers for multinationals are paid as much as $150,000 per year and sometimes more to deal with the numerous legal requirements of American firms.

In Japan the law as a profession enjoys little esteem, representing the device of last resort when two parties have failed to reach agreement through the traditional methods of negotiation. There are no more than 11,000 lawyers in Japan, one for about every 10,000 people, and they function principally as verifiers of agreements already reached. Only 500 lawyers a year are graduated from the Legal Training Institute, the only accredited law school in the country. The pay of Japanese lawyers in the early years of their careers may rise faster than that of corporate executives or journalists because the competition is less intense. After 10 years they can earn an annual salary of 7.7 million yen to 8.5 million yen ($35,420 to $39,100). However, the upper limit for the profession is normally about 10 million yen ($46,000) a year, although there are a small number who make twice that.

Japanese lawyers are now employed in greater numbers by the multinationals, often after training in Europe and the United States in the intricacies of Western international law. This new field of law is expanding the salary horizons of Japanese lawyers by exposing them to the wondrous potential—for lawyers—of Western-style legal practices and the crucial importance of the law in Western business dealings.

Indeed the frequent threat of legal action along with the payment of awesome legal fees is one of America's greatest cultural exports. The all-purpose, multitrained American lawyer, prepared to engage in any aspect of human discord subject to judicial remedy, is another American invention. These lawyers can draw up contracts, wills, purchase and sale agreements; be trustees, politicians, judges; institute or fight divorce proceedings; handle criminal and civil cases; sell the skills of entertainers, athletes and virtually anybody else under the sun.

Such a variety of tasks is traditionally shared by two types of legal specialists, barristers and solicitors, in the United Kingdom and by as many as four types in France, Italy and most of the Mediterranean countries. In Britain solicitors are the legal generalists who handle all the non-litigious work, such as contracts, wills, etc., and they generally earn less than barristers. A junior solicitor starts at about £6,000 to £7,500 ($11,600 to $14,500) a year and can go on to make £15,000 ($29,000) a year in a large commercial firm and up to £20,000 ($38,600) a year in an established law firm; he has the potential to earn as high as £30,000 to £45,000 ($57,900 to $86,800) a year in exceptional circumstances.

Barristers must join a group of more experienced lawyers at first and slowly work their way up, being assigned more cases and receiving larger shares of the fees until they can earn £25,000 to £40,000 ($48,250 to $77,200) a year. If they reach the level of Queen's Councillors, they can earn £50,000 ($96,500) or more a year. However, very few lawyers in the United Kingdom ever earn more than £100,000 ($193,000) a year and virtually none make as much as the $300,000 to $500,000 a year earned by senior partners in prestigious American firms.

Some of the highest paid people in British law are not lawyers at all but barristers' clerks. These clerks administer the affairs of groups of a dozen or so barristers who traditionally keep offices together; they take care of bills, receive and record payments and, most importantly, arrange appointments for barristers that may lead to trial or consultation work. Barristers' clerks receive a percentage of their employers' earnings, which over a year can amount to a considerable sum. In fact, so lucrative is this time-honored occupation that it is frequently handed down from generation to generation within the same family. A clerk who handles the affairs of a group of successful barristers can earn from £25,000 to £150,000 ($48,200 to $290,000) a year.

In Latin countries there are several types of lawyers who earn far more than their responsibilities would indicate to one accustomed to American or British law. For example, a *notaire* in France or *notario* in Italy has many functions, including the authorization and recording of various types of legal documents and transactions. One of the traditional and most important tasks of these legal specialists has been to lend money in the communities where they live. Their incomes from this function and other activities can be very high indeed: over 200,000 francs ($36,000) a year in France and over 40 million lire ($32,000) a year in Italy, much of which is often not declared on income tax statements. There are other types of lawyers in the two countries who handle civil problems *(civilistas* or *civilistes),* criminal cases *(penalistas* or *criminalistes),* and tax cases and commercial transactions *(commercialistas* or *commercialistes).*

The American-style all-purpose lawyer can be found in many former colonies that have retained the legal traditions of their European colonizers. As a general rule, successful lawyers in these countries earn as much as management executives in medium-size firms; for example, in Australia lawyers make from A$35,000 to A$75,000 ($39,550 to $84,750) a year and in Canada from C$80,000 to C$100,000 ($67,200 to $84,000) a year.

Judges of the high courts in all countries earn as much as top ranking civil servants and often more than the ranking government employees in noncivil service sections of the government. In the United States a justice of the Supreme Court earns $81,300 a year, and the chief justice, Warren

Burger, makes $84,700 a year. These salaries, which are higher than those of cabinet secretaries and the vice president, are slated to rise with the recent increases in federal salary schedules.

In the United Kingdom Lord Denning, Master of the Rolls, Lord of Appeal, receives £41,000 ($79,130) a year, as do the 17 other Lords of Appeal. As noted in chapter 2, only in British civil service pay schedules do the salaries in the United Kingdom match those in the United States.

In West Germany judges of the high courts make approximately 131,534 marks to 143,611 marks ($59,190 to $64,625) a year, which is a shade less than the highest civil service salary for a *Staatssekretar*. As in the United States and France, prosecuting attorneys *(Staatsanwalte)* have highly desirable jobs; while their earnings (180,000 marks [$81,000] a year, compared with about $40,000 to $50,000 a year in the United States and 225,000 francs [$40,500] a year in France) are less than those of lawyers in private practice, their jobs are secure and they have the opportunity to establish a reputation.

In Australia a chief justice earns A$91,400 ($103,280) a year, which makes him the highest paid judge in the world; the president of the Arbitration Commission, which settles wage disputes throughout the country, holds the same rank and receives the same pay.

Judges throughout the world exert more influence than virtually any other civil servant, except in countries where the law is a tool of a totalitarian or authoritarian regime. In the United States, as Chief Justice Burger pointed out, the courts have expanded the scope of their influence far beyond what was originally perceived at the time of the nation's founding. It is this recent expansion of the legal system in America that has encouraged enormous remuneration for lawyers, far greater than anywhere else in the world.

Although it is difficult to determine with great accuracy the earnings of lawyers in countries other than the United States, the incomes of physicians and dentists are even harder to pinpoint. Nowhere do doctors reveal their incomes voluntarily and in many places what they actually make is not known to their governments, their wives or even their accountants. Yet it is very clear that they make a good deal of money and that their earnings are a matter of great importance to them and to their patients. In the United States magazines for physicians in all specialties are filled with articles on the best tax shelter investments, the most tax-advantageous methods of business accounting, the pros and cons of incorporation and related subjects. (The feature article of a recent issue of a leading dental magazine discussed the quick profits to be made from buying and selling gold.)

The majority of physicians earn an average income that is in keeping with their training and the importance of their role in dealing with life and death, but the best paid are immensely overpaid in relation to the income standards for other professions wherever they live, be it Paris, Calcutta, La Paz or Chicago.

In the United States the average income for all physicians is from $69,000 to $75,000 a year, the average for radiologists, one of the highest paying specialties, is $125,000 a year and the average for dentists is about $63,000 a year. However, many physicians make less than $45,000 a year and many earn over $150,000 a year. In the United States it is quite possible for heart, brain and orthopedic surgeons to make over $500,000 a year, and a significant number of doctors earn a million dollars or more a year, although it is almost impossible to uncover their names.

In Sweden and the United Kingdom health care is entirely financed by public funds and in other European countries, it is publicly financed to a great degree. Yet in almost every country physicians have the option of practicing privately as well as treating public health care patients, and a large percentage do both or have only private patients. In the United Kingdom, general practitioners who work exclusively for the National Health Service have a guaranteed income of about £22,000 ($42,400) a year, based on their treatment of a set number of patients. Dentists average about £15,000 ($29,000) a year under the same system. In reality both types can make at least 10% to 15% more and often twice as much by treating private patients. Many doctors earn even larger sums by catering to private patients willing to pay high fees, and it is possible for a well-known physician with a list of wealthy patients to earn £150,000 to £250,000 ($290,000 to $482,500) a year.

However, most patients in the United Kingdom can only afford medical treatment through the National Health Service, and thousands who live not 10 miles from the famous Harley Street medical mecca in London go to public clinics and hospitals that may not be elegant but are efficient. Although a stiff tax is levied on their paychecks to support the National Health Service, they are entitled to receive treatment that they otherwise might not be able to afford.

The public health hospitals are staffed by younger doctors, who start at £5,400 ($10,400) a year, and, at the specialist level, by experienced physicians, many of whom care for both National Health Service and private patients.

In a study done in the 1970s of medical salaries in seven countries, Professor D. Deliege of the University of Louvain in Belgium revealed that the highest earnings for doctors were found in West Germany, followed by Luxembourg, Belgium, France, Denmark, Italy and, bringing up the rear, the United Kingdom.

As the number of physicians has risen in Europe, their incomes have declined over the past few years. Simultaneously there has been an expanded use of very complex and extensive new testing and treatment equipment. Certainly Europeans have become less inclined to go to doctors as the sophistication and expense of services have increased. Similar problems are arising in the United States, where hospitals are hard pressed to pay for some innovative diagnostic equipment and, according to the medical profession, there may be a glut of doctors in the near future. It seems that one danger of development is overinvestment in the professions and a subsequent subtle growth of underemployment among highly trained and skilled people.

Despite these small clouds on the horizon, average incomes for physicians throughout continental Europe are high. In West Germany the estimated average income for a general practitioner with an established practice, possibly one handed down from father to son, is about 175,000 marks ($78,750) a year. The incomes of dentists are almost as high, and this is generally true throughout Europe, unlike in the United States and the United Kingdom, where dentists earn somewhat less than physicians.

In France the average figure for a moderately successful doctor's practice is estimated to be 300,000 francs ($54,000) a year, and, of course, much higher in many cases. In Italy an acceptable declared income for a physician would be about 60 million lire ($48,000), but as in all European countries, it is impossible to make truly accurate estimates of the incomes of doctors and dentists because of the various diversions and subterfuges used to avoid paying taxes on total earnings.

In Japan medicine enjoys high prestige because of traditional attitudes toward the healer. Japanese doctors have one great advantage over their counterparts in other countries: they sell the medicines that they prescribe directly to their patients, often at a 100% markup. The patient in turn deducts

81

the value of the medicine on his income tax and both parties benefit greatly. Until recently even the most famous doctors in Japan made up to one-half of their income from the sale of prescription medicine. Recent revisions in the country's tax laws have diminished the profitability and thereby the extent of this activity, but it still exists. Very successful Japanese doctors can earn, from all sources of income, as much as 45 million yen to 60 million yen ($207,000 to $276,000) a year, but the median is in the range of 15 million yen ($69,000) a year.

Medicine is the best paid profession all over the world, even in countries where state-financed health systems have been devised to bring excellent medical care to everyone at reasonable prices. It would seem that health is generally more important than justice, however expensive and cherished that elusive commodity may be, particularly in the United States. Certainly the pursuit of health is far more lucrative than the search for knowledge.

6

ARTS, ENTERTAINMENT AND SPORTS

Nothing excites audiences more than the astonishing pay that sports and entertainment stars earn. This fascination with material rewards has even spilled over into those performing arts once regarded as above commerce.

In sports Dave Winfield, the baseball player for the New York Yankees and perhaps the highest paid athlete in the world, receives about $94,000 for each of his team's regular season games and, thanks to various escalating clauses in his contract, about $1.5 million a year. In the movie world Marlon Brando may hold the all-time per diem earnings record with his fee of $2,750,000 for 11 days work in the movie *The Formula*. In the performing arts opera singer Luciano Pavarotti and pianist Vladimir Horowitz command $40,000 a performance.

The phenomenal earnings of these superstars not only reflect their mass appeal but serve to increase it; what the stars earn establishes their ability to draw paying audiences almost as much as the caliber of their performances. In the

United States publicity about their earnings is geared to attract the public to see them and numerous American fans buy tickets to watch a superstar who makes a million a year just for that reason, because it is such an extraordinary sum.

Getting what you can while you can is an attitude that has always prevailed in entertainment; now it has come to dominate professional sports and is invading the arts. While the quick-buck syndrome is often perceived as an American phenomenon, it is by no means confined to the United States. People in sports and the arts the world over seek as much money as they can get, and sometimes they get more in other countries than they do in the United States. However, outside the United States earnings are not publicized for their own sake and, in fact, are usually kept secret.

In some areas of the arts European income scales have surpassed American and certainly British levels, effectively driving up the going rate for international stars. A good example of this has been the influence of the Paris Opera, particularly under the directorship of Rolf Liebermann. Utilizing an annual subsidy of nearly $30 million, the Paris Opera has bid heavily against La Scala, Covent Garden and the Metropolitan for the services of operatic superstars; all of these houses have raised their fees as much as they can, but the Met, which has virtually no official subsidy, has fallen behind in recent years. It offers a top fee of about $8,000 to $10,000 to opera stars who often get $13,000 or more at both Paris and La Scala.

Some of the major artists in both recital and concert, such as Rudolph Serkin, Isaac Stern, Itzhak Perlman and James Galway, can earn $15,000 to $20,000 per appearance, as can famous conductors, including Leonard Bernstein, Herbert von Karajan and Georg Solti. Singers Joan Sutherland and Leontyne Price command fees of $15,000 to $25,000 per performance regardless of location, be it Paris, Stuttgart, San Diego, Sydney or Tokyo. Dancers Rudolf Nureyev, Natalia Makarova and Mikhail Baryshnikov earn up to $10,000 an appearance; Nureyev's estimated annual salary is $1 million. Baryshnikov makes $150,000 a year for directing the New York City Ballet Company in addition to his fees for dancing.

Artistic and athletic stars who defect from the Soviet Union offer an interesting insight into the unique income system in the Communist world. In the Soviet Union major stars of the stage, ballet, hockey rink etc. receive top benefits because of their national and international prestige. They have fine housing, transportation, long vacations and the privilege of world travel (even if carefully supervised). Their actual monetary income is low compared to earnings in the West, but their standard of living, except for the lack of personal and often professional freedom, is very high. When they defect they trade the privileges inherent in their position for those freedoms as well as the chance to earn an income consistent with their talents. It is not so much that they are bettering their life style by leaving the Soviet bloc as trading benefits that require their dutiful presence for the freedom of a marketplace where they can make big incomes and spend them as they please.

The box-office appeal of such luminaries as Marlon Brando, Mikhail Baryshnikov or Bjorn Borg is so great that the competition for their services is carried out on a world scale and what a superstar is offered to perform in Paris will inevitably affect his fee in Chicago or Sydney.

Only a very few can be superstars in the arts, sports or any other human activity. In opera, performers of the second rank earn significantly lower fees. Singers with seasonal contracts in German state operas, called *fest* contracts, earn about 35,000 marks ($15,750) a year; the same type of arrangement at the New York City Opera pays $16,000 and at the Met $32,000. These contracts cover all performances sung plus rehearsal time.

However, most opera houses hire singers for each individual opera and pay them on a one-time basis. At the smaller houses in Europe a middle-range artist can make from 450 francs to 1,000 francs ($81 to $180) per performance in France, from about 1,500 Swiss francs to 4,500 Swiss francs ($840 to $2,520) in Switzerland and from 1,000 marks to 2,200 marks ($450 to $990) in West Germany. The fee is negotiable for leads and depends upon the reputation and performance record of the artist. The arrangements are made by the management of the house and the artist's agent, who usually gets 15% to 20% of the fee.

In the United States well-established opera stars of the second level can receive $3,000 a performance in houses in Chicago, Houston or Miami; in the larger cities of West Germany up to 6,500 marks ($2,925); and in some major cities of Italy other than Milan and Rome 4.2 million lire ($3,360).

Recitalists and performers at concerts, both vocal and instrumental, generally earn somewhat less than in opera in the United States and European countries unless they have a proven ability to draw large audiences at houses in major cities or at special regional houses. A good recital fee for a pianist, singer or other performer at Carnegie Hall in New York can run from $500 to $1,200 per performance with no expenses paid. The same performer may get 1,500 marks ($675) in Stuttgart and 3,000 francs ($540) in Grenoble.

Many American and Australian opera singers perform in West Germany and Italy and recitalists from all nations of the world appear throughout Europe, largely because of the numerous opera houses and concert halls and the receptive audiences there.

Many non-European artists who are offered bookings in

Europe must combine a number of them to make travel and living arrangements affordable, and the role of the agent or manager becomes crucial for them as it does for European, Australian and Latin American artists appearing in the United States. The world of the traveling international artist is a complex and financially intricate one involving many expenses, such as promotion, advertising and travel, that the concertgoer would probably never think of as he or she attends a performance.

Even for international artists just below the level of superstar, incomes are low considering the amount of time spent rehearsing, working and traveling. In the United States opera singers who have appeared on television, sung leads in St. Louis, Dallas and other large cities and established reputations within the business and among sophisticated fans still frequently retain "church jobs" or "temple jobs," which pay about $35 for singing at weekly services.

Both in Europe and the United States an income of $35,000 to $40,000 a year is considered excellent for the professional performing artist. A successful instrumentalist who is a member of a prestigious symphony orchestra in New York, Philadelphia or Chicago is paid a union scale of about $550 a week for a season plus pay for rehearsal time. (In addition salaries increase with longevity.) Such artists often supplement their incomes by outside playing or teaching jobs. Orchestra members in France and West Germany can earn a similar income and in the United Kingdom and Italy somewhat less.

Beneath these levels, the life of the aspiring musician or dancer is bleak and uncertain. At least 75% of the people trying to make a career in these fields are frequently unemployed.

In the theater success at the very top is usually less well paid than in music and opera. The very highest paid actors are found in the United States and the United Kingdom, and by and large these are the only countries in the world where any significant number of people can make a living as professional actors, whether in dramatic theater or in musicals. Stage stars can earn as high as $10,000 a week in the United States and up to £3,000 ($5,800) in the United Kingdom plus a percentage of the box office.

But such salaries are very rare and usually are made by such big box-office draws as Elizabeth Taylor, who earns even more, or such legendary giants of the legitimate stage as John Gielgud or Laurence Olivier. However, these people and others of their stature can make far more money by appearing in movies or on TV. For example, Elizabeth Taylor has been paid as much as $100,000 for a cameo performance involving one day of work, and Gielgud and Olivier have been making $300,000 to $500,000 for playing small roles in movies.

Below the level of major star, actors, even successful ones, are paid union scale in both countries. In the United States, an actor who belongs to Actors' Equity Association earns a minimum of $525 a week in New York, an extra earns $267.50 a week and a stage manager earns $860 a week for musicals and $735 a week for drama. In the United Kingdom the minimum for members of Actors' Equity is £95 ($180) a week for an actor and £150 ($290) a week for a company stage manager, or about one-third the rate in the United States. In addition, union members often receive supplements based on travel, type of performance, number of rehearsals and many other factors. But these minimums give a picture of the relative pay scales for professional actors in the two countries where theater is by far the most active.

For each person who gets an acting job, plays in a symphony orchestra or at a recital, sings in an opera or operetta, there are almost countless others struggling for the same opportunity. In all the arts and in entertainment throughout the non-Communist world about 90% of the money is made by 10% of the people (a situation similar to that of writers). Over 60% of the actors in Actors' Equity in both the United States and the United Kingdom are unemployed, some constantly and others most of the time. Moreover it is estimated that 75% of all actors in both the United Kingdom and the United States earn remarkably little money; the figures are £1,500 ($2,900) for the United Kingdom and $2,500 for the United States.

Movie stars are very much international commodities. When a nascent national cinematic industry suddenly experiences international success, members of that country's film industry find themselves in great demand and their earnings skyrocket to the point that they can no longer afford to work on just films made at home. The best example of this in recent years is Australia. Don McAlpine, for example, was paid $8,000 to do the cinematography for *My Brilliant Career* and a similar amount for *Breaker Morant*. Now he demands over $100,000 a film. Many other Australian actors, directors and technicians who have profited from the movie boom in that country find the opportunities and pay that go with international success taking them from Australia for much of their new work.

The same thing once happened in Italy, in Poland and, to a lesser extent, in India, where much of the local talent was drawn to the international market. Over and over, film makers who once created low-budget vehicles now work on multimillion dollar projects that must be designed to appeal to worldwide audiences in order to turn a profit. As an actor moves into the superstar status of, for example, Marlon Brando or Yves Montand, his salary and those of all the people involved in his major films mushroom, driving up the costs of making a movie. Each film becomes such a financial risk that marketability predominates in the creative process.

The nine major American film companies earn about $760 million, or some 40% of their total profits, by rentals outside of the United States and Canada. Their largest overseas markets are West Germany, France and Japan. In Japan rentals of the phenomenally successful *The Empire Strikes Back* earned $15 million and *Superman II* has proved to be another box-office smash. Needless to say, a superstar, such as Brando or Christopher Reeve, can use his or her proven box-office appeal overseas as leverage to demand even larger income.

Perhaps the highest paid people in the world are rock superstars. The biggest money earners after rock stars are probably internationally famous television and radio personalities. For example, in Australia John Laws recently signed a five-year contract for about $5 million to do his top-rated national radio program. This is a staggering sum of money for broadcast work, unmatched anywhere else except in television broadcasting in the United States. It is much more than the approximately $110,000 a year that the nationally broadcast radio star Larry King makes in America.

Television personalities in the United States make immense incomes. It is sort of a national game to guess the earnings of Johnny Carson, the talk show host so popular in the United States and so unpopular in the United Kingdom. Estimates of his income from TV work alone range from $3 million to $6 million, not counting his $250,000-a-night personal appearances and lucrative promotional deals. David Frost, Dick Cavett and Alistair Cooke, who appear on television in both the United States and the United Kingdom, have large followings but are not really entertainment superstars. Each of them earns less than $100,000 a year, although they often make more from special assignments, such as Frost's famous interviews of Richard Nixon, which reportedly earned him over $50,000.

The huge incomes of some American television stars are to a considerable degree the result of foreign showings of their series. Alan Alda makes close to $5 million a year doing M*A*S*H, which is shown throughout Europe and Japan as well as the United States, and foreign sales account for a significant portion of his income. In Europe huge salaries for television personalities are relatively rare, partly because employees of the networks are generally paid according to a government scale and partly because the star system there does not entail the enormous financial rewards found in the United States.

Each of the four members of the group Pink Floyd earn over £3 million ($5.8 million) a year and their 1980 album *The Wall* has grossed over £15 million ($29 million). Paul McCartney, probably the highest paid entertainer in the world, earned about £25 million ($48.2 million) in 1980, mostly in royalties from his hit records and songs he has written, dating all the way back to his days with the Beatles. In the past three years Kenny Rogers has earned over $10 million a year; in 1979 he made about $17 million. Popular music stars make such artists as Horowitz and Baryshnikov seem like paupers in the income sweepstakes.

Unlike the glare of publicity that surrounds the salaries of international stars in theater, films, music and entertainment, those of national sports figures are not public knowledge in any country except the United States. In fact the entire subject of what sports stars are paid in both national and international soccer, bicycle racing and even skiing is practically taboo in most of the world.

Fans know just about every detail of the million dollar, multiyear contracts for stars of American football, baseball, basketball, hockey etc. but the earnings of great world soccer players are a mystery. The reason was explained by a prominent European agent who handles many sports figures, principally soccer players, in Europe, Latin America and North America. "The first thing I tell my European clients when they come over here to play in the North American Soccer League," he said, "is that you will be bombarded with questions about how much you make. Say nothing. Don't tell the press, don't discuss it with your teammates or anyone else." In Europe, he went on, a professional athlete's official salary is merely the tip of the iceberg of his or her compensation. Many other payments are arranged unofficially to avoid taxation; in fact, the compensation for European sports stars is built to a large extent around ways of avoiding full taxation, both for the player and for the management of the team that is hiring him or her. Therefore the incomes of soccer greats are kept secret.

Occasionally figures will slip out when a sensational deal is being negotiated, often one in which a team from a certain country is trying to buy away the talents of a star from another. In 1981, the Milan team offered the Brazilian team, Flamengo, a transfer fee of $1.8 million to sell the services of Zico, the most famous Brazilian player since Pele, who was paid about $1 million a year to play for the New York Cosmos before his retirement. Zico was offered $1.2 million to sign and $1 million a year to play for three years. However, Zico loves his home and his rabid following of fans, who fill the 200,000 seats in Rio de Janeiro's Maracana stadium, the world's largest, to see him play.

With the help of Coca-Cola Brazil and the sale of some real estate holdings, Flamengo came up with enough money to keep Zico, which was $1.5 million for two years, less than the Milan offer but enough for a Brazilian patriot who wished to remain a national hero. Coca-Cola also made a deal with Zico whereby he would act as its good-will ambassador throughout the country and the company got much credit for keeping him at home. In Argentina the company has made a similar deal to keep at home Diego Maradona, an Argentine who is reputed to be the greatest player the world has seen since Pele at the age of 20. With the company's help Maradona's Buenos Aires club was able to overcome an offer from Europe by giving the young star about $1 million a year plus hidden payments.

Soccer, or football, as it is generally called in Europe, is the world's major international professional sport. In the United Kingdom stars can earn up to and sometimes over £50,000 ($96,500) a year and on the Continent as much as 500,000 marks ($225,000) a year in West Germany and sometimes as high as 75 million lire ($60,000) a year and more in Italy.

In the United Kingdom average players in the top leagues earn from £14,000 to £20,000 ($27,000 to $38,600) a year; on the Continent they make somewhat more. Consequently many British players labor in other European countries for better money, as do many Latin Americans. However, while Brazilians play in Spain, Belgium or Italy, for example, none of the Europeans play in Latin America.

In recent years a number of European and Latin American players have come to the United States to play with teams in the North American Soccer League. It is testimony to the strength of European habits, customs and fear of taxes that their salaries have for the most part remained secret even under the scrutiny of the American press. Some incomes slip out during moments of stress; Johan Neeskens, the great Dutch star, was earning $300,000 when he was with the New York Cosmos. Giorgio Chinaglia is reputed to earn from $400,000 to $600,000 for the same team, and other European stars make in the range of $200,000 to

FIVE TOP MONEY MAKERS IN MEN'S AND WOMEN'S WORLD TENNIS (1981)

Men		Women	
John McEnroe	$941,000	Martina Navratilova	$865,437
Ivan Lendl	$716,037	Chris Evert Lloyd	$572,162
Jimmy Connors	$395,872	Tracy Austin	$453,409
Guillermo Vilas	$387,261	Andrea Jaeger	$392,115
Jose Luis Clerc	$317,375	Pam Shriver	$366,350

$300,000 playing for various American teams. With few exceptions European players earn more in the United States than they would at home.

Other major sports with principally international audiences are tennis, golf and boxing. Horse racing is both national and international, but the majority of the money is bet and won within individual countries. Table 1 lists the five leading money makers in both men's and women's tennis in 1981 and Table 2 presents the same information for golf.

Skiing is another very important sport in Europe and North America where the earnings of the athletes are virtually impossible to determine. Like tennis and golf, the income from sponsoring equipment is a large part of the earnings of a successful skier. In fact the more a sport permits participation by the average fan the more income can be generated by commercials, sponsorships, subsidiary arrangements and personal appearances. Bjorn Borg is estimated to have made almost $3 million in this fashion in

FIVE TOP MONEY MAKERS IN MEN'S AND WOMEN'S WORLD GOLF (1981)

Men		Women	
Tom Kite	$375,699	Beth Daniel	$206,978
Raymond Floyd	$359,360	Joanne Carner	$206,649
Tom Watson	$347,660	Pat Bradley	$197,050
Bruce Lietzke	$343,446	Donna Caponi	$193,917
Bill Rogers	$315,411	Jan Stephenson	$180,529

1981, and while the figures are not available, the earnings that skiers Jean Claude Killy and Ingemar Stenmark receive for sponsorships are considerable indeed.

It is estimated that one-third of the entire population of France comes out to watch the racers in the famous Tour de France, perhaps the most commercialized athletic event of them all. This race is the premier cycling event in Europe and winners or members of winning teams can expect lucrative sponsorship deals and assured appearances in local races throughout the Continent for years. In these races stars of the Tour are assured of victory by prearrangement, and they are in effect paid by the local authorities—a chamber of commerce, a cycling club, a regional fair committee—to enhance the event. For each one-day appearance in the year following victory in the Tour it is possible to make 50,000 francs ($9,000), and earnings for a year can be spectacular for individual cyclists, who make more than winning players in the World Cup soccer competition.

The two great superstars of the Tour de France are Eddie Merkx, a Belgian, and Bernard Hinault, a Frenchman. Merkx is a legend in Belgium and besides his appearances at local races, which have continued for years since his final Tour de France victory, he does a vast amount of promotion for cycling equipment. His estimated annual income has been put as high as 100 million Belgian francs ($3 million). Hinault is a three-time winner of the Tour de France and his appearances in local races combined with his sponsorships yield him at least 6 million francs ($1.08 million) a year. Members of teams who appear in races with him are guaranteed daily purse earnings of 10,000 francs to 15,000 francs ($1,800 to $2,700).

In recent years hockey has grown from a regional sport, played mostly in Canada and the United States, to an international attraction. Hockey stars in Canada and the United States now command salaries approaching $1 million a year and, in the case of the phenomenal Wayne Gretzky, even more. In Sweden, Finland, West Germany, Norway and Switzerland local teams, theoretically amateur, give their players side jobs and benefits as well as under-the-table salaries. A North American of average ability can make as much as $30,000 to $45,000 a year playing in some European countries. Coming the other way, Swedes, Finns and even Czechs now play in North America. The famous Swedes Anders Hedberg and Ulf Nilsson both make about $500,000 a year playing for the New York Rangers, and several Czechs have defected from their country to play in North America for salaries of $100,000 a year and more.

Other examples of transplanted sports are baseball and basketball. In Japan some players make 16 million yen ($73,600) or more a year, and the great Sadaharu Oh, who hit a career total of 800 home runs, made a base salary of 54 million yen ($250,000) in 1981, his last year. Basketball, another American export, is now played in European and Asian countries. However, incomes in these countries are lower than in the United States, where it is the highest paid professional sport. Some American players, however, earn $40,000 to $60,000 a year in Europe.

There are several sports in which the line between amateur and professional is blurred, and often a sport has become professional when that distinction ceased to exist. This is what happened with tennis. It is almost hard to remember the days when Wimbledon was an amateur event, since it has now become such a money slugfest. Track, particularly the modern marathon, is another, though less notable, example. The day is not far off when flycasting, ping-pong, log rolling and any other activity that involves competition and attracts enough of an audience to warrant commercialization will become a professional and eventually an international sport.

7

THE MEDIA:
Publishing and
Journalism

Every year in Canada, France, West Germany, Italy, the United Kingdom, the United States and many other countries where the written word is held dear, young university graduates, educated in literature, history, philosophy, social and cultural studies, seek jobs in book, newspaper and magazine publishing. Bright, alert and highly motivated, they make the rounds of the publishing houses in their respective countries: Scribners in the United States, Weidenfeld and Nicolson in Britain, Gallimard in France, Mondadori in Italy, Elsevier in the Netherlands and numerous others, both large and small, in publishing centers around the world.

A majority of them are in for a financial shock. Many seek any job they can get in publishing and so many apply that only a very few can be hired and then often for extremely low salaries. In the United States an assistant to an editor might start at $8,500 to $9,000 a year; in the United Kingdom anywhere from £4,500 to £5,300 ($8,700 to $10,200); in France perhaps around 55,000 francs ($9,900); in Italy about 12 million lire ($9,600). In West Germany, after an arduous apprenticeship, a starting editor can make from 24,000 marks ($10,800) a year. In many cases they are offered less money than postal workers, manual laborers, police officers, commercial secretaries, factory workers and numerous other categories of job holders.

The same situation exists in most other aspects of publishing, such as marketing, publicity, design and production. In sales departments the annual starting pay is somewhat higher: from $14,000 to $16,500 plus 10% commission in the United States; from about £5,000 to £7,500 ($9,600 to $14,500) in the United Kingdom; and from as high as 85,000 francs to 90,000 francs ($15,300 to $16,200) in France. Nevertheless in most countries publishing jobs are few and far between, and the beginning salaries are so low that not many can survive on them without taking second jobs, living poorly or having other financial resources.

Because of the cost of maintaining people on staff (social security and unemployment benefits, health insurance etc.), many publishers use free-lancers for various editorial and design tasks, such as proofreading, copy editing and jacket design. A free-lance copy editor makes about £3 ($5.80) to £3.50 ($6.75) an hour in the United Kingdom, $7 to $9 an hour in the United States and about the same in France; proofreaders generally earn slightly less. Considering the lack of benefits, these rates are significantly lower than the hourly wages paid to workers in numerous areas of manufacturing and construction. A jacket designer in France averages about 3,000 francs ($540) for a job, which is about the same as the scale in the United States and Canada; in Australia the rate is somewhat lower.

Publishing has a reputation of paying poorly, and in general it is well deserved. Why is this so? Partly it is because the educational systems in the developed countries turn out more students trained in the humanities and related fields than there are jobs to be filled. Too many qualified people compete for too few jobs and the exigencies of the marketplace take their toll both in the number of openings and the salaries offered. It is estimated that about half of the editors in West Germany have PhDs. College graduates who go into other fields, such as business or engineering, start at considerably higher salaries, as much as 50% higher in some cases in most of the countries mentioned.

But why are newly graduated humanities majors willing to work for such low wages? The single most important reason is that publishing is both interesting and prestigious. While it is a serious business, publishing in most countries is neither very businesslike nor very profitable, but it does offer the pleasures of working with the written word. In addition there is the opportunity to work with highly identifiable and unique products and a continuously changing group of authors; the chance to market such products; and the possibility of discovering great talent and/or books of major worth.

Salaries in the middle and upper-middle range in publishing, while clearly lower than those in manufacturing, are more competitive with those in other fields. A senior editor in France can make 195,000 francs to 250,000 francs ($35,100 to $45,000) a year, in West Germany from 50,000 marks to 75,000 marks ($22,500 to $33,750) a year. In Italy a senior editor at a major house, such as Rizzoli, can earn as much as 72 million lire ($57,600) a year; in the United Kingdom a similar position pays £18,000 ($34,700) a year; and in the United States the pay is from $45,000 to $60,000 a year.

The same pattern occurs in other areas of publishing. A director of production in France earns from 200,000 francs ($36,000) a year at a medium-size house to as much as 325,000 francs ($58,500) a year at a large publisher; in the

United Kingdom about £12,750 ($24,600) at a medium-size house; in Italy from 36 million lire to 42 million lire ($28,800 to $33,600) at a larger publisher; in the United States about $30,000 to $33,000 at a medium-size publisher; and in Australia A$28,000 ($31,640) at a medium-size house. A director of publicity in France can reach a salary level of 210,000 francs to 230,000 francs ($37,800 to $41,400) a year; in the United Kingdom about £12,000 ($23,100) a year; in the United States $35,000 to $40,000 a year; and in Australia A$25,000 ($28,250) a year. A director of sales in France might earn from 200,000 francs to 225,000 francs ($36,000 to $40,500) a year at a medium-size house and 275,000 francs ($49,500) at a large publisher; in the United Kingdom £12,750 ($24,600) a year at a large house; in the United States from $50,000 to $65,000 a year at a major publisher; in Australia A$35,000 ($39,550) a year at a larger publisher; and in Canada about C$45,000 ($37,800) a year at a larger house. All these salaries are below those for jobs with equivalent responsibility in other industries in the countries cited.

At the very top—chief executive, operating officer or, in some cases, owner of the house—the salaries suddenly are competitive or even higher than those paid by firms in other industries with similar sales volumes, including chemicals, textiles, banking and manufacturing. For example, in the United States a chief executive in a firm that manufactures electrical equipment with annual sales of $100 million to $150 million averages about $170,000 a year with salary and bonus. A chief executive in one of several publishing houses with the same sales makes about $180,000 a year (or 20 times as much as an assistant to an editor in the same house and about 15 times as much as a secretary in the firm).

In France, where many publishing firms are family owned or have been under the same directorship for extended periods, the annual salary range for a publisher at a small house is 420,000 francs to 500,000 francs ($75,600 to $90,000); at a medium-size house 540,000 francs to 625,000 francs ($97,200 to $112,500); at a large and diversified house, such as Hachette, 950,000 francs to one million francs ($171,000 to $180,000). (At a similarly diversified, very large house in the United States, McGraw-Hill, the president, Harold McGraw, made $347,000 in 1980 in salary alone.) These salaries are slightly less than average for equivalent positions in French industry.

In the United Kingdom the head of a publishing firm can make £30,000 to £45,000 ($57,900 to $87,000) a year, and if he also owns the house, he can of course make far larger sums, as much as £100,000 ($193,000) or, in rare cases, more, including salary and a share of company profits. In West Germany the head of a publishing house usually makes less, from 125,000 marks to 165,000 marks ($56,250 to $74,250) a year, plus considerable fringe benefits.

Salaries paid by publishing houses in Europe, North America and Australia are low at the bottom and middle and become more competitive at the higher end, but only in the United States do chief executives earn as much or more than their counterparts in other industries. Because of the low starting salaries and the limited opportunities for advancement, a career in publishing has become steadily less attractive in all the countries mentioned for those lucky enough to get the jobs. An amazingly large number of young people who begin as assistants or secretary/assistants in various aspects of publishing move on to some other field when they discover that the present is financially unrewarding and the future is fiercely competitive.

Prospects for advancement always exist, of course, for highly talented and tenacious workers, but the number of openings for senior editors, publicity directors, sales managers, marketing directors, production managers and their higher ranking assistants is too small to accommodate the pressure from below for promotion. The high turnover presents an inconvenience but not a great problem for management; there is always another philosophy graduate from Yale or Oxford or the University of Rome or Toronto who is eager to start work immediately for a relatively meager salary. And some will remain despite the vicissitudes.

This continues to be true even as publishing has been forced to change in order to survive in a competitive market with other media, principally television and its new cable variations. Because of rising production and labor costs, more copies of each title must be sold to earn a profit and the search for massive best-sellers drains considerable money and energy from the pursuit of worthier literary products for a more discriminating audience. Publishing companies are frequently acquired by conglomerates in search of quick glamour and profit and later dropped, to be picked up by another huge concern. Job insecurity is a way of life for the staffs of publishing houses.

When a book does well, in the original hardcover edition followed by a significant paperback and movie or television sale, then the place for the author to be is in the United States. This is true in the case of first authors, such as Betty Lord, whose publisher had the foresight to give her novel, the best selling *Spring Moon,* special treatment before publication and was able to sell the paperback rights for over $400,000. It is also true in the case of established lions of the commercial literary marketplace, such as Carl Sagan, who received a $2 million advance based on merely the outline of a novel in 1981 that is still only an outline at the beginning of 1982.

Other major sales in the United States were Avon's purchase of the paperback rights for *Elvis* by Albert Goldman for $1 million. Both hardcover and paperback rights to the same book were sold in the United Kingdom for £180,000 ($347,400). The paperback rights for Thomas Harris' *Red Dragon* were sold to Bantam (owned by the West German conglomerate Bertelsmann) for $1.65 million; all rights to the same book were bought in the United Kingdom for £115,000 ($221,905). The sales figures for these books indicate the relative difference in the size of the commercial markets in these two major publishing countries.

Staggering incomes for established authors and sudden windfalls for neophytes excite publishers and the public in all countries. Some authors—for example, Guenter Grass, Alberto Moravia, Gabriel Garcia-Marquez, Harold Robbins, Irving Wallace and Morris West—have enormous popular followings both at home and abroad. Many of these authors have earned a million dollars and a few of them have made much more over the years, with reprints and movie or TV treatments of their books.

However, in all the major publishing countries discussed, over half the books published do not make any money at all, and many actually lose money. In France less than one hundred authors earn a full-time living through their writing. Many writers are also professors; five of the recently acclaimed 10 most influential living French authors—Raymond Aron, Claude Levi-Strauss, Michel Foucault, Fernand Braudel, and Bernard-Henri Levy—are teachers as well as authors. Others are editors in publishing houses, an old French tradition with such famous examples as Andre Gide at Gallimard. Some are even politicians; President Francois Mitterand is the author of nine books.

Similarly, in the United Kingdom few writers make a full-time living at their trade, working as journalists, editors, professors (to a lesser extent) and whatever else is available to supplement the generally paltry incomes from book sales. Because of the high prices of books, print runs of 5,000 copies or even less can make a respectable profit for the British publisher of a book intended for a general audience. Such a small number would generally be a financial flop in the United States and, to a lesser extent, in other European countries. Thus books on topics normally considered too specialized for publication in the U.S. trade market are regularly put out in Britain, enriching the literary fare but maintaining the "precipice mentality" that has pervaded many publishing houses in the United Kingdom during recent years.

A study made in the United States in 1981 titillated the publishing world there with the statistically proven conclusion that the average author earns less than $5,000 a year. In a survey of 2,239 authors 10% made $5,000 a year or more and the remaining 90% earned less than $5,000, averaging $4,775 a year. The median hourly rate for authors was $4.90, which is considerably below the average manufacturing worker's wage. However, it must be remembered that writing is one of the highly competitive entrepreneurial fields in which success comes very hard and failure is frequent. By no means do more than 10% of the aspirants in professional sports or in films, theater, dance, opera or any of the other arts make a financial success of their careers.

One of the hardest ways to earn a living in publishing is by being a free-lance writer for magazines and newspapers. Many book writers attempt to supplement their incomes in this manner, as do editors at publishing houses in West Germany, Italy and, particularly, France. A free-lance writer in West Germany, by writing for various outlets, can make from 50,000 marks to 60,000 marks ($22,500 to $27,000) a year, but this is very rare and higher than what free-lancers in other European countries generally make.

In the United Kingdom and the United States earning a

living by free-lance writing has become practically impossible for all but exceptionally prolific, and often well-known, writers. Considering the time and effort put into writing an article, magazines pay very little, ranging from about £120 to £350 ($232 to $676) in the United Kingdom and from $750 to $2,500 in the United States. In order to earn a gross salary of $30,000 a year, a writer must sell at least 15 to 20 articles to high-paying magazines, an extremely difficult feat to accomplish. It can be done, however, although after professional expenses and normal costs of living the writer's net income generally amounts to less than one-third of his or her gross earnings before taxes.

Editors who work for magazines usually earn more than their counterparts in book publishing, particularly in the case of newsmagazines. In West Germany an editor at *Der Spiegel* earns from 50,000 marks to 90,000 marks ($22,500 to $40,500) a year. A managing editor at a newsmagazine in West Germany makes from 120,000 marks to 150,000 marks ($54,000 to $67,500) a year plus generous benefits. In the United States editors for *Newsweek* and *Time* earn only slightly more than West German newsmagazine editors: from $45,000 to $75,000 a year. Writers for newsmagazines in the United States are paid about $25,000 to $60,000 on the average.

In the United Kingdom newsmagazines, such as the *Economist,* will pay from £11,000 to £15,000 ($21,200 to $29,000) a year at the top. Editors and writers for entertainment and special-interest magazines earn quite a bit less in most countries; the salaries paid by theater and arts magazines in West Germany average about 50,000 marks ($22,500) a year; in the United Kingdom the same type magazines pay about £8,000 ($15,400) to £10,000 ($19,300) a year. In the United States the highest editorial salary at one of the most successful women's magazines is $26,000 a year.

Newspaper employees generally do not make as much as those who work for newsmagazines. The exceptions are columnists and long-established editors and reporters. In virtually all countries the staffs of newspapers are highly unionized and the complex rate schedules for salaries at different levels are often the subject of major industrial disputes. This is particularly true in the United Kingdom, where in addition to confronting management the numerous independent unions representing many different job categories at newspapers are at times even in conflict with each other. As a result of financial and labor difficulties, several newspapers have gone under and such famous papers as *The Times* and *The Sunday Times* have at times been in danger of going out of business; both newspapers were shut down for almost a year in 1978-79 because of a labor dispute.

The salaries for editors, reporters and writers are negotiated separately at each of the major British newspapers. Average salaries at the *Financial Times, The Guardian* and *The Times* range from £10,000 to £14,000 ($19,300 to $27,020) a year; the tabloids, such as *The Sun* and the *Daily Mirror,* pay the highest salaries, starting at £11,500 ($22,195) a year and going up to £15,000 ($28,950) or more a year. Journalists who work for the provincial newspapers are paid considerably less; the minimum at papers with a circulation of 30,000 to 150,000 is about £6,000 to £7,500 ($11,580 to $14,475) a year.

In the United States the pay at major urban papers, such as the *New York Times,* the *New York Daily News,* the *Chicago Tribune,* the *Chicago Sun-Times* and the *Los Angeles Times,* varies somewhat according to location, but not a great deal. The *New York Times* pays its domestic correspondents and editors a minimum of approximately $590 a week, or $30,680 a year; bureau chiefs and desk heads

make about the same. Reporters, copy editors, photograph-
ers and news make-up staff start at about $540 a week, or
$28,080 a year.

Many of the journalists on these papers make more than
the minimum. In both the United Kingdom and the United
States journalists who work for the major newspapers have
several years of previous experience. They are considered
the pick of the crop of their profession.

The national average for beginning journalists throughout
the United States is about $14,500 a year and can reach
$25,000 to $30,000 a year for desk editors at the smaller
metropolitan dailies, such as the *Trenton Times* or the *Des
Moines Register*. The salaries for managing editors in the
United States average about $40,000 a year, with a high of
$180,000 a year paid by a major Eastern daily and a low of
$13,000 a year reported at a recent managing editors' con-
vention. The average salary for managing editors at smaller
metropolitan dailies is $50,000.

In Australia reporters and editors at the major dailies in
Melbourne and Sydney are grouped into four classifications:
A, B, C and D. The lowest rung, D, earns from A$220 to
A$250 ($249 to $283) a week, or A$11,440 to A$13,000
($12,948 to $14,716) a year; C averages A$300 ($339) a
week, or A$15,600 ($17,628) a year; B earns from A$360
to A$370 ($407 to $418) a week, or A$18,720 to A$19,240
($21,164 to $21,736) a year; and A makes about A$450
($509) a week, or A$23,400 ($26,468) a year. In addition a
"surplus" can be paid to the best reporters and columnists,
which can add as much as A$400 ($452) a week, or A$20,800
($23,504) a year, so that the top paid journalists in Australia
can earn as much as $50,000 a year. Such salaries are very
rare, but they do exist and indicate that journalism can be a
relatively high paying profession in Australia. Managing
editors at the largest urban papers, however, make less than

their counterparts in the United States, earning from A$80,000 to A$90,000 ($90,400 to $101,700) a year.

The same is true in Japan, where journalists enjoy more prestige than in most other countries. The Japanese honor communications in general and the written word in particular, and the country has one of the highest newspaper circulations per capita of any country in the world and several of the largest dailies in the world. A career in journalism is considered more prestigious than such professions as medicine and, certainly, law. In fact journalists are held in the same esteem as high government officials and corporate executives and wield a similar amount of power. At the major urban newspapers a top journalist or columnist can earn 17.5 million yen ($80,000) a year. The average salary of a newspaper employee in Japan is about 4.45 million yen ($20,470).

In West Germany the salaries of newspaper journalists are definitely lower than those of their colleagues at newsmagazines. A top editor at one of the Springer papers can make 100,000 to 150,000 marks ($45,000 to $67,500) a year. Reporters and editors at major papers, such as the *Frankfurter Allgemeine Zeitung,* earn from 36,000 marks to 45,000 marks ($16,200 to $20,250) a year, and managing editors rarely earn more than 85,000 marks ($38,250) a year plus substantial fringe benefits. Many newspaper journalists supplement their income by writing magazine articles and books, and some hold part-time jobs.

According to the Syndicat de la Presse Parisienne, minimum annual salaries at dailies in the Paris area for journalists with 10 years' experience are 200,500 francs ($36,090) for editors in chief; 130,000 francs ($23,400) for bureau chiefs; 110,000 francs ($19,800) for chiefs of writers, editors and photo reporters; 95,745 francs ($17,234) for reporters; and 68,575 francs ($12,344) for beginning copywriters and copy editors. Of course, there are many who make more than the minimum for their particular level. Also, as in New York, London and other major cities of the world, employees of the large papers have all had previous experience, generally making far less for several years working in smaller cities and towns around the country.

Journalists' salaries in France are lower than those of journalists in Australia, Japan and the United States. They are also somewhat lower than the salaries in West Germany and Britain but within the general range of pay scales for journalists in the major media countries, very much as is the case with book and magazine publishing.

In China, the official stated salary for editors at the *People's Daily* is 250 yuan ($143) a month, or 3,000 yuan ($1,716) a year, a sum that means more in the overall scope of salaries than by itself. Thus an editor at a major newspaper makes about the same as one of the numerous vice ministers in the government but less than a university professor, who officially earns 322 yuan ($185) a month, or 3,864 yuan ($2,220) a year.

Probably the greatest disparity in journalistic salaries is in the area of television journalism. The role and income of the American TV "anchorperson" on both network and regional news programs are truly unique. Dan Rather of CBS earns $800,000 a year, Tom Brokaw of NBC close to a million a year and Jessica Savitch of NBC about $600,000 a year. There are also many anchorpersons both on national and local news programs who average about $250,000 to $300,000 a year. Why these staggering salaries are paid is something of a mystery, even to the management of the networks themselves.

News programs have enjoyed a larger and larger following recently. It is said that if an anchorperson is able, through his or her charisma or personal appeal, to raise the percentage of people watching his or her program by only one point, the network will realize several millions in increased advertising revenue. In addition the hype surrounding the salaries paid to these people becomes self-fulfilling; the more outrageous an anchorperson's salary is, the more people watch him partly in awe of that salary, thereby increasing the network's profitability.

TV reporters in the United States can earn from $60,000 to $90,000 a year and some make $100,000.

In no other country do the salaries paid to TV journalists even approach those earned by anchorpersons and many reporters in the United States. In France, West Germany, Italy, the United Kingdom, Canada and Japan, the salaries of on-camera people are sometimes higher than those of writers, technicians, directors and producers, but not a great deal. It is unlikely for a West German anchorperson to earn much more than 100,000 marks ($45,000) a year, and a British anchorperson for the BBC makes no more than £17,000 to £20,000 ($32,800 to $38,600) a year. ITV, Britain's commercial television, pays somewhat higher but still far less than salaries in the United States.

At the BBC, union scale for cameramen is about £8,562 ($16,500) a year and the heads of news and current affairs departments make a top salary of £28,000 ($54,000) a year. Controllers earn up to £35,000 ($67,600) a year and the highest paid executives of the BBC staff make about £35,000 to £40,000 ($67,600 to $77,200) a year.

Nowhere else do the salaries in TV journalism match those paid by the networks in America, and it is in this field that the single largest paycheck anomaly between the United States and other countries exists.

8

INDUSTRIAL AND OFFICE WORKERS

From the moment of his arrival in another country, a traveler quickly becomes aware, at least in a general way, from little details as well as stark contrasts with his own country, of the working conditions and general standard of living in his new environment. The attitudes of workers toward themselves and others and the way they act both in their jobs and socially will frequently tell a lot more about how much they are paid and how they live than any amount of statistics.

The average monthly wage of a factory worker in India was about 1,000 rupees ($110) in 1981, compared to an average monthly wage in France of about 4,738 francs ($853) for a factory worker. In other words, the Indian made about one-eighth as much as his counterpart in France. Yet this enormous imbalance in pay scales hardly begins to reveal the vast difference between the standard of living in the two countries.

The longer I sought to compare incomes the more I was struck by how many ways the disparities between the developed and the less-developed countries and their economies manifest themselves. Physical contrasts are stunning, sometimes terrifying, and the structure of social organization is often evident at the airport—at customs, taxi stands, street signs.

Appearances can also be extremely misleading. Travelers to New York are invariably struck by the dirt and trash on the streets, including the famous Times Square area, and in public places, such as parks, subway stations, etc. Can it be that the United States is really a poor country? Indeed, the populace seems incapable of providing the labor necessary for such a basic amenity as cleanliness.

A sanitation worker in New York City makes about $18,000 a year, which is about three times the income of the chief of staff of the Indian Army; yet many overpopulated cities in Asia are neater. The New York sanitation man makes more than 14 times the annual wage of 1,500 pesos ($1,200) earned by a street sweeper in Havana, Cuba. Furthermore the American has street-cleaning equipment that would stagger the imagination of his counterpart in Havana. But even the Cuban street sweeper makes twice as much as an unskilled worker in Dacca, where the average annual wage is 5,000 rupees ($532), or in Peking, where the average annual urban wage is 800 yuan ($456).

Can it then be a problem of overdevelopment? Are American municipal workers so highly paid that New York cannot afford to keep enough of them and their equipment working? In Geneva the annual salary for similar municipal work is about 34,000 Swiss francs ($19,000), and in London it's about £5,000 ($9,650). New York is in the upper range of these salaries if allowances are taken for the recent increased value of the dollar; yet Geneva and London are definitely cleaner.

It is essential to remember in these discussions that the varying standards of living can make monetary comparisons of incomes misleading. The salary of the Indian Army chief of staff buys more in India than the salary of the sanitation worker in New York, especially considering the perquisites the general receives. However, the paycheck sums are values in real convertible currencies and comparisons are applicable for that reason. The sanitation worker could save $6,000 in one year and go to New Delhi, to live like a general for a while.

The explanations are complex and involve allocation of resources, which register the relative importance placed on public appearances, and the degree of pride that citizens take in their habitat. There is apparently less such pride in New York, an observation that can lead to risky speculation about a declining sense of community and the effects of harsh ethnic and social conflicts on general orderliness and the appearance of the city. (Actually, as far back as de Tocqueville, New York was noted for its filth.) The dirt of New York is not the dirt of poverty per se, but the indifference of a relatively affluent populace can be just as unpleasant to see as that of an impoverished one.

These subtleties notwithstanding, obtaining information on the widest range of salaries is, for many reasons, generally easier in a country where the standard of living is higher. Educational levels are higher, social services are more extensive, and for better or worse, there is a greater coherence and similarity of functions within the society, which a stranger can more swiftly recognize. Organized accessibility to basic information is one of the keys to learning anything about a new country and is indispensable when the subject is as complex and variable as the economy.

Finding out what workers earn in developed countries has become a sophisticated science that provides governments with essential information to guide, or misguide, them in formulating economic policy. In the advanced nations statistics reveal what workers earn in every conceivable industry and enterprise. Changes are carefully plotted, in some cases weekly and even daily, and the number of workers— male and female, full and part time, regular and seasonal— are analyzed. Altogether a great deal more information is compiled than could possibly interest very many people other than economists.

For example, I can assure you from figures supplied by the European Community that in 1979 an average worker in the footware industry in France made 15.68 francs an hour ($2.82), in Italy 2,241 lire ($1.79) and in the United Kingdom £1.59 ($3.07). This sort of information and much more like it is available for about 30 countries in the world; a fair amount of more limited information concerning workers' incomes is generally available in another group of about 30 countries. Concerning the remaining countries of the world, there is either some crude data, which is compiled by the International Labor Office, or no data at all.

A variety of sources indicate that the daily wage of a skilled industrial worker in Bangladesh is about 35 takas ($1.97), 195 sucres ($6.83) in Ecuador and 2.16 naira ($3.43) in Nigeria. These figures and similar data for other less-developed countries are valuable for comparative purposes, but what they actually tell is questionable. Most sources available vary widely in their figures, and the International Labor Office's *Yearbook of Labor Statistics* is unavoidably two or more years older, depending on the time it takes to gather and publish the complex data and the uncertainty of the information available in many less-developed countries.

Many jobs, particularly in less-developed countries, do not have a formal structure and are paid by various means, including barter, exchange of services, food, clothing, and shelter. Sometimes there is no payment at all, as in the case of involuntary labor or slavery. Since it is almost impossible to develop statistics in many such situations, the ILO must use whatever data is available. Nonetheless it is interesting to compare payscales in less-developed countries based on what information exists. Table 1 is drawn from a number of sources, the principal one being the *Yearbook of Labor Statistics, 1980.*

Except for Costa Rica, all the countries shown in this table rank in the poorer half of the nations of the world in terms of gross national product, but they all had sufficient statistical resources and a desire to contribute data to the International Labor Office for its *Yearbook of Labor Statistics.* There are many countries in the poorer half of the world that either do not have any data on incomes or do not choose to submit such information. Among them are Gabon, Ghana, Guinea, Mali, Sudan, Uganda and Zaire in Africa; Guadeloupe, Haiti and Paraguay in the Americas; and Afghanistan, the People's Republic of China, Indonesia, Iran, Iraq, Laos, Vietnam, the Yemen Arab Republic and the People's Democratic Republic of Yemen in Asia. These and still other nations without any income data represent a very sizable portion of the earth's population which toils for wages that cannot be analyzed or compared.

Some say that it is even harder to find out how much an Italian doctor makes than it is to discover the income of a Polish Communist Party bureaucrat or that the profits of an Eskimo fur trader are easier to learn than the wages of a Bolivian tinworker. But these statistics involve relative difficulties in areas of some sophistication. The greatest problems exist where the workers and their conditions are so isolated or primitive in their activities that no sensible comparisons can be drawn.

Somewhat higher up the ladder are those countries— often, though not always, wealthier—for which reasonably complete data are available. Table 2 shows the annual aver-

Table 1

ESTIMATED ANNUAL WAGE* OR SALARY* OF
NONAGRICULTURAL WORKERS IN 17 LESS-DEVELOPED COUNTRIES

Area	Country and Year of Data		Local Currency	U.S. $ 1982 Equivalent
Asia	Bangladesh	1977	3,011 takas	$ 169
	Jordan	1977	596 dinars	$1,800
	Philippines	1979	5,105 pesos	$ 613
	Sir Lanka	1980	4,337 rupees	$ 211
Africa	Algeria	1977	9,855 dinars	$2,346
	Burundi	1979	100,008 francs	$1,111
	Egypt	1976	339 pounds	$ 492
	Kenya	1978	1,339 pounds	$ 134
	Malawi	1978	670 kwacha	$ 744
	Nigeria	1979	743 naira	$1,179
	Zambia	1977	1,656 kwacha	$1,882
Latin America	Bolivia	1978	35,592 pesos	$1,424
	Costa Rica	1978	25,248 colones	$1,262
	Cuba	1977	1,740 pesos	$2,175
	Honduras	1978	4,032 lempiras	$2,016
	Nicaragua	1977	14,362 cordobas	$1,436
	Peru	1979	234,592 soles	$ 469

*As interpolated from latest available data on hourly, daily, weekly and/or monthly incomes of workers in nonagricultural sectors (all job fields other than farming, fishing and forestry) and based on 52 weeks.

116

age income, interpolated from ILO statistics and other sources, of workers in manufacturing and industry in 10 of these middle countries. It might seem surprising at first that India and Pakistan, which according to their gross national products are among the poorest nations of the world, maintain a sophisticated and relatively inclusive statistical capability. While their poverty stems to a great extent from overpopulation, they both have a fairly modern administrative apparatus that operates more efficiently than that of many richer nations.

Although the data is several years old in most cases, it represents the latest internationally collected information and is therefore the most useful for comparative purposes. It should be remembered, however, that change has occurred in the past few years; upward in the case of India, for example, and downward in the case of Bangladesh.

The economic systems of Communist nations are different from those of the rest of the world in terms of fixed rates of exchange and wage-price structures, which are established by the government. Accurate statistics on earnings in these countries are difficult to obtain; the People's Republic of China and Vietnam have yet to report income data to the ILO.

Table 3 shows the estimated annual income of factory workers in eight Communist countries.

The official currency rates in Communist economies are always subject to alteration in a real bargaining and trading situation vis-a-vis other countries. Within the countries themselves, particularly the Soviet Union, much remuneration is given in the form of material advantages; money has less convertible power and less actual use for the citizens. This, of course, is less true in such Eastern European countries as Poland and Hungary, where there is private land ownership and a significant degree of private enterprise.

Table 2

AVERAGE ANNUAL WAGE* OR SALARY* OF
MANUFACTURING WORKERS IN 14 DEVELOPING COUNTRIES

Area	Country and Year of Data		Local Currency	U.S. $ 1982 Equivalent
Asia	Burma	1978	2,544 kyats	$ 394
	India	1977	5,604 rupees	$ 616
	Pakistan	1976	4,660 rupees	$ 476
	Syria	1977	5,720 pounds	$ 1,459
Africa	Morocco	1979	5,720 dirhams	$ 1,077
	Mauritius	1979	4,976 rupees	$ 465
	South Africa	1978	4,020 rand**	$ 4,221**
			9,664 rand***	$10,147***
Latin	Brazil	1976	34,128 cruzeiros	$ 273
America	Colombia	1980	23,010 pesos	$ 460
	Chile	1980	94,368 pesos	$ 2,359
	Mexico	1980	114,612 pesos	$ 4,584
	Panama	1977	2,723 balboas	$ 2,723
	Uruguay	1979	47,976 new pesos	$ 3,838
	Venezuela	1978	22,440 bolivares	$ 5,161

*As interpolated from various sources, including the *Yearbook of Labor Statistics, 1980,* and based on 52 weeks.
**Total population.
***White population only.

Table 3

AVERAGE ANNUAL WAGE* OR SALARY* OF
MANUFACTURING WORKERS IN EIGHT COMMUNIST COUNTRIES

Country and Year of Data		Local Currency	U.S. $ 1982 Equivalent
Bulgaria	1980	2,244 leva	$2,412
Czechoslovakia	1980	30,660 korunas	$5,286**
Germany, East	1979	12,024 marks	$5,344***
Hungary	1980	45,000 forints	$1,286
Poland	1979	64,800 zlotys***	$ 810**
Rumania	1979	25,416 lei	$5,686***
Yugoslavia	1980	73,200 dinars	$1,864
USSR	1979	2,092 rubles	$2,827

*As interpolated from various sources, including the *Yearbook of Labor Statistics, 1980.*

**Based on official government exchange rates effective Jan. 1, 1982.

***The figures for Poland are based on data supplied for 1979 before the political unrest and economic disorder altered the salary structure through inflation. The official rate of 31 zlotys per dollar in 1979 was not realistic then, nor is the official rate of 80 zlotys per dollar now, when the actual rate is more like 350 to 400 zlotys per dollar. Incomes have fluctuated wildly to keep up with the decline in the value of money. Therefore in all probability no firm figures for earnings will be available for the contemporary situation for some time.

119

Virtually all the salaries in the Communist countries cited are for workers in state-owned industries. In addition these workers receive a variety of social benefits, including basic medical care, education and, in some cases, housing. Certain additional advantages can accompany rank or political position. In fact, perks based on complicated refinements of the political hierarchy are well known in many Communist states, as pointed out in the previous chapter. The existence of corruption and the "black economy" is legend in Poland, Czechoslovakia, Hungary and perhaps most of all in the Soviet Union.

Each country has its own system of perks, which are usually related to the principal scarcities of the individual economy. In Poland and some other countries in Eastern Europe more and better quality food and drink are accorded to the privileged. In China one notices that the simple Mao jacket comes in a range of different qualities of cloth and cut that would challenge the abilities of a tailor on Savile Row, each grade being a signal that its owner is "more equal" than those wearing a poorer garment.

It is also true that the black economy becomes increasingly active and widespread the further the "official rate" of a currency strays from any relevance to the real value of goods. Again in regard to clothing, Western observers are impressed by the stupendous prices (as much as $400 for a pair) that foreign-made blue jeans fetch in countries such as Hungary, Yugoslavia, Rumania and even the USSR, a phenomenon reflecting both adoration of capitalist "knicknackery" and the softness of the local currency when confronted with demand for a limited product whether imported legally or smuggled.

Ascending the ladder of developed countries and larger annual incomes, it is striking to note the old paradox that communism exists in countries with a low industrial level,

quite contrary to the historical societies of Marx and the socialist doctrine of the 19th century. This can be seen by comparing
the incomes of the states in the West, Japan and Oceania with
those of the Soviet bloc and other socialist countries.

Average income is a barometer of a country's gross national
product and general standard of living, and in all three
categories Japan and the wealthy Western nations are far in
the lead of the rest of the world and appear to be constantly
widening the gap. This is clearly one of the causes of conflict between the rich-poor, North-South, developed-devel-
oping axes. The question that exacerbates international
economic relations is whether the rich nations increase their
superior economic position at the expense of and because of
the relative poverty of the less-developed countries. Although
the question cannot be solved here, the contrasts illuminated
by the disparities in income shown emphasize the terrible
severity of the problem.

A comparison of average annual manufacturing incomes
in the industrialized countries is a complex affair because of
the additional value and costs of remuneration not included
in direct pay. For example, in five countries of Western
Europe in 1976 social security and related fringe benefits,
including overtime and bonuses, comprised the following
percentage of labor costs and total value of worker remuneration: England 28%, Sweden 37%, West Germany 40%,
the Netherlands 43% and France 44%. In other words, above
and in addition to the direct pay sums these fringe benefits
must be added to give a complete picture of the total value
of the pay package.

Other guaranteed benefits accrue to workers in most highly
developed societies, including in some cases additional
money for each dependent, cost of living increases, unemployment benefits, medical and educational allowances, travel
allotments and longevity raises. Among the most significant

benefits or guarantees for workers in some of these economies is the existence of a minimum legal wage. The size of this wage indicates the relative affluence of the societies. In the highly industrialized countries the annual minimum wage represents many more times the average yearly wage or salary in the developing nations shown in Tables 1 and 2 of this chapter.

In the United States the current hourly minimum wage is $3.35, or about $6,968 a year based on a 40-hour week. In Canada the minimum wage is C$3.50 per hour, or about C$7,280 ($6,115). In France it is 3,078.40 francs a month, or about 36,940.80 francs a year ($6,649). In the Netherlands the minimum wage for workers over 23 years old is 1,925.30 guilders per month, or about 23,103.60 guilders ($9,472) a year.

In the United Kingdom, West Germany, Belgium and Japan there is no general minimum wage. However, each industry in these nations has an established minimum pay scale; in the United Kingdom it generally varies from £59 a week, about £3,068 ($5,921) a year, to £70 a week, about £3,640 ($7,025) a year. It is interesting that the aforementioned minimum wages are about equal in all highly developed countries.

The most highly industrialized non-Communist nations are generally regarded to be Argentina, Australia, Belgium, Britain, Canada, Denmark, France, West Germany, Greece, Ireland, Israel, Italy, Japan, the Netherlands, New Zealand, Norway, Sweden, Switzerland and the United States. All but Argentina are members of the Organization for Economic Cooperation and Development (OECD) and nine belong to the European Community. Other countries qualify as highly developed, but only those already mentioned, except for Argentina and Spain, are included in Table 4, which compares the annual average manufacturing income (average of all industries) of each.

Table 4

AVERAGE ANNUAL WAGE* OR SALARY* IN MANUFACTURING
(AVERAGE OF ALL INDUSTRIES) IN 18 DEVELOPED COUNTRIES

Country and Year of Data		Local Currency	U.S. $ 1982 Equivalent
Australia	1981	A$ 9,256	$10,460
Belgium	1980	BF 449,680	$13,990
Canada	1981	C$ 17,732	$14,895
Denmark	1980	DKr 113,621	$15,907
France	1981	FF 61,600	$11,088
Germany, West	1981	DM 33,119	$14,904
Greece	1980	Dr 268,800	$ 5,376
Ireland	1980	I£ 4,825	$ 7,670
Israel	1980	Shekel 40,908	$ 2,454
Italy	1980	Lira 8,176,000	$ 6,540
Japan	1980	Yen 3,568,423	$16,415
Netherlands	1979	Gld 31,164	$12,466
New Zealand	1980	NZ$ 10,816	$ 8,869
Norway	1980	NKr 94,080	$15,994
Sweden	1980	SKr 84,000	$15,120
Switzerland	1981	SF 31,282	$17,518
United Kingdom	1981	£ 5,782	$11,159
United States	1981	$ 16,226	—

*Based on 52 weeks except countries that pay for 56 weeks. Bonus added in average where relevant. Figures are exclusive of overtime and computed on average hours worked.
Sources: Eurostat, *Hourly Earnings, Hours of Work, 1980*; International Labor Office, *Yearbook of Statistics, 1980*; *OECD Economic Outlook*, no. 29, July 1981; and various newspaper and magazine articles, reports and interviews.

123

It must be remembered that these comparisons are for annual wages or salaries averaged over all industries in each country. The incomes for agriculture are generally much lower in each nation and those for mining of energy products, selected areas of heavy industry and automobile manufacturing are much higher. These differences will be covered in the following chapter for workers in both developed and less-developed economies.

The salary comparisons presented in Table 4 follow quite closely the pattern of compensation for management discussed in chapter 4, "Executives and Managers," except for the anomaly of the very high executive incomes paid to top management in the United States. These executive salaries are not matched by correspondingly larger wages for American workers. In fact, in several countries higher wages are paid to workers for labor and in a number of others wages are equal or nearly equal to those earned in the United States.

The spread between the highest paid executive and the average worker is greater in the United States than in many other countries. Again let's compare Sir David Steel's salary of £120,385 ($232,000) as chairman of British Petroleum in 1979 with Robert O. Anderson's salary in 1980 of $1,650,000 (£858,000) as chairman of the equivalent-sized Atlantic Richfield. Sir David made about 17.5 times as much as the average employee's £6,881 ($13,280). Anderson made 45.9 times as much as the higher average salary of $23,000 for a petroleum worker in his company. The earnings spread between the two oil company chairmen, of course, decreases and, in some cases, even turns the other way as the comparison of salaries descends to middle and lower-middle management; several other industrialized economies have more advantageous salary scales than found in the United States.

In recent years a crucial consideration in analyzing manufacturing salaries has been the total cost of the employee to the firm and the worker's productivity. Productivity has become a word used with almost mystical ardor, as the Western world stands in awe of the extraordinary efficiency of Japanese manufacturing and the competition it offers to the other industrialized nations. In this regard automobile manufacturing is the most publicized at the moment. The question of relative productivity and salary levels in that area is taken up at length in chapter 10, "Transportation Workers."

In every facet of the industrial process the productive capacity of the workers and their machinery and equipment is essential to an understanding of wage comparisons. Figures presented by the OECD for the period 1975-80 concerning increases in both productivity and labor costs in six developed countries are revealing. Japan had the highest rise in productivity—7%, followed by Italy 5.5%, France 4.5% and West Germany 3%. Japan also had the lowest rise in labor costs—1.5%, followed by West Germany 3.5%, the United States 6.5%, France 8% and the United Kingdom 15%.

These comparisons show that Japanese labor produced more units of manufacture for less money than all the other countries and that the workers in the United Kingdom had practically no increase in output while costing 15% more to employ over the same period of time. I do not mean to imply that the workers are the only ones responsible for success or failure. The productivity of an industrial complex involves management, labor, government, the economy, the international trading situation and many other things as well as wages and other incentives. One very important element, however, is the attitude of the workers; whether they believe in rewards for performance and in fact receive them—as in Japan—or are skeptical about the remuneration they will actually be able to enjoy for increased effort in an inflation-bound economy, such as in the United Kingdom.

Productivity and income go hand in hand in most cases, but not always. American automotive workers are the highest paid but not the most productive; British automotive workers are the poorest paid and the least productive. High productivity is a result of many factors besides pay; it depends on value judgments about work, about one's employer and about one's general role and purpose in society. It also depends on the skill of management, the social and educational milieu in which both employer and employee have been raised and even a sense of personal and national prestige. It can perhaps be argued that either very high or very low wages militate against productivity and, ultimately, job security, as evidenced by the example of automotive workers in the United States.

Another way of examining the incomes in highly industrialized countries is to compare the salary scales of different types of office employees. Table 5 presents the salaries of receptionists, bilingual secretaries and executive secretaries in eight countries: six Western European nations, the United States and Japan. In most cases the pay for secretarial jobs is at least equal to or, at the top, much higher than the average manufacturing wage in each country; some exceptions are noted after the table.

Once again, the salaries follow the same national pattern as those of industrial workers and middle management; office work in the United States is comparatively well paid at the upper-middle and top levels in relation to Western Europe and Japan. (The salaries for secretarial and office workers in the less-developed countries are discussed in the chapter on multinational corporations.)

In conclusion, the immense discrepancy between work-

126

Table 5

ANNUAL SALARY FOR THREE OFFICE JOBS IN EIGHT COUNTRIES (1981)

	RECEPTIONIST			BILINGUAL SECRETARY			TOP EXECUTIVE SECRETARY		
		Local Currency	U.S. $ 1982 Equivalent		Local Currency	U.S. $ 1982 Equivalent		Local Currency	U.S. $ 1982 Equivalent
Belgium	BF	455,000	$13,650	BF	520,000	$15,600	BF	650,000	$19,500
Germany, West	DM	29,000	$13,050	DM	36,400	$16,380	DM	41,600	$18,720
Japan	Yen	1,200,000	$ 5,520	Yen	3,500,000	$16,100	Yen	5,000,000	$25,300
Netherlands	Gld	27,900	$11,439	Gld	32,500	$13,325	Gld	41,200	$16,892
Norway	NKr	72,000	$12,240	NKr	80,000	$13,600	NKr	105,500	$17,935
Switzerland	SF	32,000	$17,920	SF	37,500	$21,000	SF	52,000	$29,120
United Kingdom	£	4,325	$ 8,347	£	6,500	$12,545	£	7,400	$14,282
United States	$	10,900	—	$	21,000	—	$	24,500	—

Source: Manpower, Inc. and its European Division, headquartered in Paris, France, have provided much of this information.

ers' pay in the developed and the less-developed countries is readily apparent, and it is almost impossible to conceive of the gap ever being closed. In a world in which the average manufacturing wage for one year is 25 times greater in the United States than it is in the Philippines, for example, or the salary of a receptionist in Switzerland is 13 times as much as that of a factory worker in nearby Rumania, the measurement of human existence in terms of paychecks alone would be staggering as well as misleading in its implications.

This difference is even greater when earnings in agriculture are examined; out of the hundreds and hundreds of millions who live off the land, many barely survive, while some prosper. The chastened conclusion of a traveler seeking to make global comparisons of how the myriad workers fare is that we live in not one but many worlds in terms of comfort, identity and freedom to enjoy activities other than working all the time. We must always bear in mind that the vast majority of people in the world works just to subsist.

9

AGRICULTURE, MINING AND PETROLEUM WORKERS

In a remote hill district of Nepal, where subsistence farming is the main activity, the annual income of farmers is $7; the wealthiest among them earn $60 a year. The inhabitants can grow crops during only four months of the year because they have neither the technology nor the resources to irrigate their land during the dry months between October and July. These Nepalese live near some of the most beautiful mountain ranges and scenery in the world; yet their existence is one of desperate poverty, as the appalling figures about their incomes demonstrate. Their lives are shackled to an earth they cannot make productive and their energy remains unused for much of the year.

This extreme example attests to the fact that agriculture is the lowest paying of all mankind's enterprises and is at the bottom of the income scale in almost every country regardless of economic development, even though the production of food is the most essential occupation of all.

In much of the Southern Hemisphere and in less-developed lands elsewhere, millions of people till the soil for no monetary reward, being paid for their labor with shelter, food and clothing or the produce they harvest. Some work for nothing at all, living at the whim of landowners in fixed, traditional relationships, and some are still in a state of outright slavery.

Outside of Western Europe, most of the Communist nations and North America, there are surprisingly few countries that have more workers in manufacturing than in agriculture. These include Argentina, Australia, Israel, Japan, New Zealand and Uruguay. Hong Kong, Singapore, Taiwan and some of the United Arab Emirates, which have little or no arable land, are in the same category. Thus the vast majority of the world's workers are engaged in its lowest paying occupation. Moreover, as a general rule, the higher the proportion of farmers there are in a country, the poorer it is in terms of standard of living and per capita gross national product.

Even in the most highly developed countries, where there are proportionally fewer farmers in the labor force, agriculture is still the lowest paying profession. In Belgium, for example, an average farm worker made about 332,024 Belgian francs in 1979 ($8,853). While he earned about 1,265 times as much as his impoverished counterpart in Nepal and is one of the highest paid farmers in the world (see Table 3), he made only a bit more than half as much as a Belgian coal miner, who earned an average 586,640 Belgian francs ($15,801) that year.

In almost every country of the world these two general occupations, agriculture and the extraction and processing of energy from the earth, represent the extreme ranges of workers' incomes. The tables in this chapter will prove this point by examining workers' incomes in 10 less-developed countries, five Communist nations and 12 developed nations.

The two occupations, although disparate in numbers of workers and remuneration, have several intriguing factors in common. When shoe manufacturers or bookbinders go on strike, the reaction is one of minor annoyance. When transport workers, air controllers or steelworkers walk off the job, the economy staggers but rights itself and is able to continue despite intense disruption. But when farmers stop producing food, miners stop supplying coal or the flow of oil is cut, nations grind to a halt. Farmers and miners have overthrown governments and changed the course of history for many centuries; they continue to do so to this day. Miners strike in Poland and shake the foundations of the state, peasants revolt in Latin America and topple governments, OPEC threatens the world with oil embargoes and financial markets panic. These are familiar headlines.

Incomes and productivity in agriculture, mining and petroleum strongly influence the domestic politics of countless countries and are becoming a dominant factor in international relations as the sources of fossil fuel grow more scarce and the production or distribution of food continues to fall short in large areas of the world. Surging population growth combines with these scarcities to disrupt the international economy. Ironically even in the areas where the food supply is overabundant, such as in North America and Western Europe, the political problems related to agriculture are just as divisive and intense.

Each year in the United States the system of price supports given to the enormously productive agricultural industry is a prominent source of contention for the government, Congress and the public. This strife is a major fact of political life in the country that exports more food per capita than any other. On the other hand, low food production in the USSR and other Communist countries, having become almost endemic, is a continuous economic drain and a cause of political unrest. Farm income and the problem of balancing agricultural price supports in a fiercely competitive situation constantly threaten the stability and future of the European community.

The threat of miners' strikes over wages places immense pressure on governments attempting to balance budgets. This is dramatically true in Britain. Despite their relatively small numbers, only 351,000 in 1979, the miners have brought down more than one British government, and it is generally acknowledged that what the miners settle for in pay increases sets the stage for the labor-management wage battle throughout the entire nation and can determine the future of the incumbent government.

In Poland striking coal miners (only 413,950 in 1979) bolstered Solidarity in its efforts to reform wage and living conditions throughout the nation and offered the strongest resistance to the government's crackdown in December 1981. Everywhere coal miners and other workers involved in energy development and production have political power well beyond their numbers in the population. From the earliest days of the Industrial Revolution they have been politically active and frequently in conflict with governments and political systems. (In recent history they have used their power to defend the status quo from time to time in some countries, as the success of their agitation brought them the highest laboring wages to be had in those nations.)

Production of food and energy are indispensable in every nation, but the less developed the country the more human resources are required to grow crops and the less money the farmers are able to get for their products. Table 1 shows the average annual incomes of agricultural and mining workers in 10 less-developed countries and the percentage of the work force engaged in agriculture and manufacturing in these countries.

In countries where the standard of living and workers' incomes are very low, such as Cameroun and Malawi, a vast majority of the work force is engaged in agricultural systems with very poor productivity levels. The same is true to somewhat less an extent in the rest of the countries in Table 1 and, indeed, in a number of the other less-developed countries. More people work growing less food in these countries than elsewhere. The vision of mankind shrugging off the chains of agricultural subsistence in order to develop varied and more viable economies remains an unfulfilled dream for most of the nations of the earth.

Regardless of how little developed a country may be or how crude its mining industry may be, the salaries of mining workers are anywhere from twice to five times as much as those of farmers. General manufacturing incomes are also much higher than earnings in agriculture, but the difference is notably less than it is in comparison with incomes in the mining industry, which pays the highest. A worker elite is often formed in urban and industrial areas within basically agricultural societies, and the disruptions that this causes to family, tribal and traditional life add a new burden to the society. Many more men are available for mining and manufacturing than there are jobs, a situation that tends to create large groups of urban unemployed. The siren of enormously higher wages unsettles social patterns and can outweigh the benefits of new capital and opportunity being injected into the economy of a developing country.

Table 2, which examines earnings in five Communist countries, shows a similar but less striking gap between agricultural and mining incomes. In these countries the income of miners is always less than twice as much that of farmers.

133

Table 1

AVERAGE ANNUAL WAGE OR SALARY OF AGRICULTURAL AND MINING WORKERS IN 10 LESS-DEVELOPED COUNTRIES, AND PERCENTAGE OF ACTIVE WORK FORCE ENGAGED IN AGRICULTURE AND IN MINING

| | AVERAGE ANNUAL WAGE/SALARY | | | | % OF WORK FORCE ENGAGED IN | |
| | Agriculture | | Mining | | | |
	Local Currency and Year of Data	U.S. $ Equivalent*	Local Currency and Year of Data	U.S. $ Equivalent*	Agriculture	Mining
Cameroun	11,100 francs 1976	$ 40	52,957 francs 1979	$ 186	73.8	4.5
Costa Rica	9,724 colones 1979	$486	18,072 colones 1979	$ 904	NA	NA
El Salvador	1,560 colones 1979	$624	3,850 colones 1978	$1,540	41.0	14.5
India	1,260 rupees 1979	$139	8,575 rupees 1979	$ 943	53.5	5.8
Malawi	187 kwacha 1978	$208	359 kwacha 1978	$399	84.4	4.7
Nicaragua	7,250 cordobas 1978	$725	17,846 cordobas 1978	$1,785	42.0	16.2

	Local Currency and Year of Data	U.S. $ Equivalent*	Local Currency and Year of Data	U.S. $ Equivalent*		
Pakistan	3,900 rupees 1979	$398	9,120 rupees** 1979	$ 931	53.9	13.4
Philippines	2,250 pesos 1977	$270	4,803 pesos 1977	$ 576	48.7	10.9
Sri Lanka	2,640 rupees 1978	$129	8,556 rupees 1979	$ 417	50.1	9.3
Syria	2,172 pounds 1978	$557	7,540 pounds 1978	$1,933	31.9	15.6

*1982.
**Mining and manufacturing.
Sources: International Labor Office, *Yearbook of Labor Statistics, 1980; The Statesman's Year-Book 6, 1981-82;* George Thomas Kurian, *The Book of World Rankings;* and various articles, newspaper reports and interviews.

135

Table 2

ANNUAL AVERAGE SALARY OF AGRICULTURAL AND MINING WORKERS IN FIVE COMMUNIST COUNTRIES, AND PERCENTAGE OF ACTIVE WORK FORCE ENGAGED IN AGRICULTURE AND MINING

| | AVERAGE ANNUAL SALARY | | | | % OF WORK FORCE IN | |
| | Agriculture | | Mining | | | |
	Local Currency and Year of Data	U.S. $ Equivalent*	Local Currency and Year of Data	U.S. $ Equivalent*	Agriculture	Mining
Bulgaria	1,879 leva 1979	$2,088	2,661 leva 1979	$2,957	NA	NA
Czechoslovakia	30,264 korunas 1979	$5,218***	43,620 korunas 1979	$7,521***	NA	NA
Hungary	39,072 forints 1979	$1,116	68,268 forints 1979	$1,950	21.7	34.2
Poland	61,776 zlotys 1979	$ 772***	111,804 zlotys 1979	$1,398***	30.2	29.1**
USSR	1,752 rubles 1979	$2,368***	3,146 rubles 1979	$4,251	NA	NA

*1982.
**Mining and manufacturing.
***Based on official government exchange rates effective Jan. 1, 1982.
Sources: International Labor Office, *Yearbook of Labor Statistics, 1980; The Statesman's Year-Book 6, 1981-82;* George Thomas Kurian, *The Book of World Rankings;* various articles, newspaper reports and interviews.

This in some measure can be attributed to the fact that agriculture is largely a state enterprise with partially regulated incomes; it is also more productive and employs fewer people than is the case with the countries in Table 1. Efforts have been made by some Communist governments to maintain a degree of balance between earnings in agriculture and in the higher paying industries, particularly where the abandonment or inefficient use of farm land has already had disastrous effects on agricultural production. Cuba, for example, has made great efforts to keep agricultural income as close as possible to earnings in industry.

Nevertheless agricultural production on state-owned and -operated farms has been one of the greatest economic failures of the Communist system, and food shortages that debilitate and disarrange an economy have cursed Soviet and Polish development, to name two leading examples.

The general economic development of the countries shown in Table 2 is far higher than that of the nations in Table 1, and as would be expected, the ratio of farmers to miners is evened out. In fact, in Hungary and Czechoslovakia more workers are engaged in mining and manufacturing than in agriculture. As perceived through a comparison of incomes with those in the less-developed nations and those in the highly industrialized capitalist countries, the countries in Table 2 can be viewed as being in a middle phase of economic development.

Table 3 considers earnings in 12 developed countries, where the income levels for both the agricultural and mining sectors are far higher than in the countries listed in Table 1 and Table 2. The earnings gap between the two sectors remains quite evident. Most of the countries in the table— the United States, the United Kingdom, Japan, Canada and Australia—maintain about a two-to-one or greater ratio between the pay of mining and farm workers. In Belgium, the

Table 3

GROSS AVERAGE ANNUAL SALARY OF AGRICULTURAL AND MINING WORKERS IN 12 DEVELOPED COUNTRIES, AND PERCENTAGE OF ACTIVE WORK FORCE ENGAGED IN AGRICULTURE AND MINING

| | AVERAGE ANNUAL SALARY | | | | % OF WORK FORCE IN | |
| | Agriculture | | Mining | | | |
	Local Currency and Year of Data	U.S. $ Equivalent*	Local Currency and Year of Data	U.S. $ Equivalent*	Agriculture	Mining
Australia	A$ 7,800 1979	$ 8,814	A$ 12,833 1979	$14,501	6.7	1.2
Belgium	BF 420,000 1979	$12,600	BF 547,441 1979	$16,423	2.9	0.7
Canada	C$ 8,016 1979	$ 6,733	C$ 20,343 1979	$17,088	5.0	1.6
France	FF 38,265 1979	$ 6,888	FF 53,296 1979	$ 9,593	8.2	0.7
Germany, West	DM 14,625 1979	$ 6,581	DM 30,343 1979	$13,654	5.9	1.2

	Local Currency and Year of Data	U.S. $ Equivalent*	Local Currency and Year of Data	U.S. $ Equivalent*		
Ireland	I£ 2,956 1979	$ 4,730	I£ 4,829 1979	$ 7,726	19.0	0.7
Italy	Lira 5,686,720 1979	$ 4,549	Lira 6,822,400 1979	$ 5,457	13.5	24.3**
Japan	Yen 1,305,000 1979	$ 6,003	Yen 3,179,376 1979	$14,625	13.6	0.2
Netherlands	Gld 27,270 1978	$11,180	Gld 35,381 1978	$14,506	5.6	0.1
Sweden	SKr 66,528 1979	$11,975	SKr 102,157 1979	$18,388	5.7	0.3
United Kingdom	£ 4,165 1980	$ 7,997	£ 8,049 1980	$15,454	2.5	1.3
United States	$ 9,264 1981	—	$ 21,837 1981	—	3.4	0.9

*1982.

**Mining and manufacturing.

Source: Eurostat, *Hourly Earnings, Hours of Work, 1980*; International Labor Office, *Yearbook of Labor Statistics, 1980*; *The Statesman's Year-Book 6, 1981-82*; George Thomas Kurian, *The Book of World Rankings*; and various articles, newspaper reports and interviews.

Netherlands and Sweden the income levels are definitely closer, largely because of the extreme degree of protection afforded farmers in these countries.

A comparison of the three tables in this chapter demonstrates the extraordinary decline in the percentage of farmers in the work force with the advancement of economic development. Furthermore, as a result of the increased productivity achieved through mechanized and modernized agricultural methods, far less people can grow much more food, a phenomenon most striking in the United States and Canada. However, in these countries, the paragons of farming efficiency, agriculture is one area where incomes have not advanced in line with productivity; the United States, for example, outproduces many countries whose farmers are considerably better paid than are American farmers.

Leaving the farm for the city is not only the fashion in the less-developed societies of Africa, Asia and Latin America; the same process has been occurring in North America for many years. The growth of huge agribusinesses and larger farms owned by individuals combined with advances in technology and farming methods have increased efficiency while reducing the need for labor. There is less incentive than ever to keep the worker on the farm, and so away he goes to the bright lights.

The figures in Table 3 help to indicate why agriculture has become the source of great political conflict in the European Community. Although the United Kingdom and West Germany are the two most efficient agricultural producers, they have low farmer incomes compared with those of the other community countries listed in the table; they also have a low percentage of labor engaged in farming (the United Kingdom's percentage of workers engaged in agriculture is the lowest in the European Community). Italy has proportionally five times as many workers in agriculture and Ireland six times. France also has a significantly higher number of farmers in relation to its total work force.

The existing price support system in the European Community encourages increased production of food, which is to the advantage of the more agricultural countries, such as Ireland, Italy and France. The community's agricultural policy for all member governments sets the prices for main farm products each year and buys all unsold products at these prices, placing levies on imported food to raise their prices to community levels. Since the United Kingdom and West Germany have small, though highly efficient, farming sectors and must import large amounts of agricultural produce, they, in effect, are subsidizing the greater output of countries with larger, overproducing agricultural industries. For example, in 1980 Italy earned about $800 million in farm profits and France even more, while the United Kingdom contributed about $800 million to the community budget, much of it in the form of price supports, and West Germany almost $2 billion.

The politics of agricultural overabundance is a problem for developed nations, but for the majority of countries around the world the problems are scarcity of food and low incomes. Thus, both the high productivity of agriculture in advanced economies and the opposite situation in the poorer nations can cause political tension and, in Africa, Asia and Latin America, turmoil.

The high incomes of mining workers in all parts of the world reflect the fact that the extraction of energy requires relatively few workers and that the output is limited and essential to all economies. Paradoxically the very high miners' incomes in the United States, Japan and Western European countries are no longer matched by increasing productivity, since in many cases the energy sources have been drilled for so long that they are near depletion or are much more difficult to reach and exploit. For this reason increases in salaries in the energy industries, protected by union contracts, are often accompanied by actual declines in the production of coal, natural gas and oil. Such a situation can lead to stagnation and even a decline in the overall energy productivity of advanced countries and a situation where rising workers' incomes contribute directly to inflation.

The three tables in this chapter comparing workers' incomes in the highest and the lowest paying industries delineate the progress of economic development from such poor nations as Malawi to the wealthy nations of the West and the advanced economies of Asia. They show the changing number of people who toil in farming, which is everywhere the least financially rewarding enterprise. Yet I have only been dealing with the statistically identifiable workers in agriculture. Millions more plant and hoe in places where life is too crowded or to remote to analyze.

10

TRANSPORTATION WORKERS

The majority of the inhabitants of the globe live out their lives without ever leaving one small area, probably less than 50 miles from end to end. This monotonous reality is easy to overlook when much of the history we are taught is measured in unique voyages of discovery, resettlements of populations and dramatic treks by armies and entire peoples across thousands of miles. Yet travel as an integral part of everyday life is a very recent development. In industrialized societies the whirl of people constantly on the move, hurrying off somewhere only to return quickly, commuting back and forth from work or play, is very much a phenomenon of the modern era.

The number of people on the move today—in airplanes, trains, buses, cars—is awe inspiring, providing jobs for millions of workers. What can explain the necessity of so many people traveling so many miles? The most satisfactory answer is a new variant of Parkinson's Law: the more accessible and convenient travel becomes, the more essential it becomes. Businessmen fan out every day to every part of their own countries and to the farthest reaches of the globe to attend conferences, make deals, examine markets and facilities, have lunch and dinner, sell and buy products and commodities on a face-to-face basis.

Well over half the space on airline flights is occupied by expense account travelers going somewhere to talk with someone and achieve something that in earlier days was done by letter, cable or phone. Consequently a stagnant or declining world economy has immediate negative effects on transportation workers as businesses retreat to more frugal, older methods of conducting their affairs. Indeed, a thinning out of people at the travel terminals and on the byways is currently threatening the livelihoods of millions of workers throughout the industrialized world.

The same variant of Parkinson's Law applies to pleasure and vacation travel. Cars and buses streak over miles of road bringing people to somewhere different for a day, a weekend, a week; planes bear vacationers across mountain ranges and oceans for a brief period away from home. Travel is the thing to do if you can possibly afford it; no one wants to get left behind.

There are many types of travel, from the simplest subway ride to a jaunt on the space shuttle. Altogether they finance many of the world's paychecks.

In the modern world perhaps the epitome of mechanized man is the bus driver. References to him, jokes about him, criticisms of him, quotations from him and interviews with him are a rich vein of modern folklore. His job exists where-ever there is a road network, which, at one extreme, can be gleaming ribbons of concrete or, at the other extreme, dirt tracks. Generally the bus driver's paycheck is higher in the more developed nations, but the importance of his job can often be greater where poverty is significant and travel hard and uncertain.

144

Table 1 lists the annual gross incomes of bus drivers in various places around the world, all stated in dollars. The figures are for a period from 1979 to 1981; there is an error factor of (±) 10% due to changes in pay, regional economic fluctuations, currency disruptions and other problems. Unfortunately, it is impossible to give actual net incomes or their buying power in these cases. Nevertheless I think this table gives a broad picture of how bus drivers around the world are paid.

Taxi drivers are another category of transportation workers found in rich and poor countries alike. Cab drivers in developed countries, for example, can earn 20% or 30% more than bus drivers if they work long hours and are conscientious. A good income for a cab driver in London would be around £140 ($270) a week after expenses, and someone who owns or shares a cab in New York could earn $500 a week. The variations in fares and earnings in the taxi business are enormous, particularly so in developing countries, where cabs are a luxury for the rich.

Bus drivers are usually in the middle range on the pay scale of employees in mass transportation; railway engineers generally earn more and brakemen, conductors, signalmen and maintenance people earn less. The highly skilled craftsmen who repair transportation vehicles usually receive better pay everywhere.

Bicycles are essential in China and other developing nations, cargo ships distribute goods over the entire globe and trains are reassuming their earlier role as the most important mode of mass transportation; yet the health of most advanced national economies rests to an uncomfortable degree upon the profitability of General Motors, Toyota, BL Ltd. (formerly British Leyland) or Volkswagen, to name a few of the biggest auto manufacturers. The economic viability of the primary producing nations—those that sup-

145

Table 1

ANNUAL GROSS SALARY OF BUS DRIVERS
AROUND THE WORLD
(Adjusted for Period from 1979-1981)

	Annual Gross Salary in U.S.$
Abu Dhabi, United Arab Emirates	9,161
Amsterdam, the Netherlands	17,900
Athens, Greece	6,450
Bangkok, Thailand	2,095
Bogota, Colombia	1,916
Buenos Aires, Argentina	3,952
Caracas, Venezuela	8,323
Dublin, Ireland	8,682
Duesseldorf, West Germany	21,000
Helsinki, Finland	11,856
Hong Kong	4,800
Istanbul, Turkey	3,473
Johannesburg, South Africa	8,263
London, England	9,577
Luxembourg City, Luxembourg	21,497
Madrid, Spain	8,323
Manila, Philippines	1,796
Mexico City, Mexico	4,910
Milan, Italy	10,100
Montreal, Canada	14,970
New York, United States	19,250
Oslo, Norway	15,210
Panama City, Panama	2,574
Paris, France	15,250
Rio de Janeiro, Brazil	4,371
Singapore	2,574
Stockholm, Sweden	14,790
Sydney, Australia	11,736
Tel Aviv, Israel	8,263
Tokyo, Japan	15,688
Vienna, Austria	14,011
Zurich, Switzerland	25,508

Sources: International Labor Office, *Yearbook of Labor Statistics, 1980;* Union de Banques Suisse, *Prix et Salaires dans le Monde (1979-1980);* and reports, newspaper articles and publications of various government agencies.

ply such raw materials as iron ore, rubber, bauxite—depends on them as well and upon the major manufacturers of aircraft and aircraft parts and, indirectly, the airlines.

Of the major transportation industries, motor vehicles and airlines have received the most public attention in recent years, both because they are cornerstones of the international economy and because they have suffered serious financial reverses, which have affected the paychecks of vast numbers of people in both the developed and less-developed nations. In fact, it is frequently because of the income structures built around these two industries that economies are in difficulty.

"Frankly," said a senior executive of Nissan Motors in Tokyo to the visiting head of the United Auto Workers (UAW) union, "I think that it is very difficult for people who make $6.17 an hour to buy a car which is being made by a worker who earns $12.65 an hour." The Japanese executive's statement hit on one of the reasons why Japan sells autos to the United States instead of the other way around.

The comment was made in 1981, when the price of a typical Japanese car, delivered in the United States, was about $1,500 lower than the cheapest American model. This situation, so ruinous to the U.S. auto industry, was the result of lower labor costs and higher worker productivity in Japan; the same problem was also facing auto manufacturers in Western Europe. The gains in salary and benefits that had been won by the auto workers' union over years of struggle combined with energy shortages, tight credit and high interest rates now hung like a millstone around the neck of the American auto industry. The onslaught of competition from Japan, a unique, consensus society organized in "company unions" and armed for an international trade war with a dazzling will to win, put Americans out of work, shrank the market for both domestic and European-produced cars and inflicted severe damage on the world's largest economy.

While vehicle production in the United States rose 9% from 1975 to 1979 and declined slightly in Western Europe, Japanese production rose by 36% during those years. Japan has become the largest producer in the world, followed by the United States (several million units behind), France and West Germany (a distant third and fourth). Meanwhile the American auto industry has been forced to lay off workers and cut production; 1981 was the industry's worst year in two decades.

In 1980 world production of passenger and commercial vehicles was about 40 million units, and a slow annual increase to about 45 million units in 1985 is predicted. In today's automobile market the cutting edge has become price and the cost of operation and maintenance. The manufacturer who can produce the cheapest vehicles to buy, operate and maintain will succeed.

Table 2 compares total hourly labor costs, direct hourly wages and direct annual wages for workers in four major auto-producing countries in 1981. Labor costs are defined as the employer's costs for all social and fringe benefits plus actual direct wages.

Although a British worker's salary is clearly the lowest, comparative studies at two virtually identical Ford plants, one in Halewood, England, and the other in Saarlouis, West Germany, showed that it still cost approximately $1,000 more to manufacture a car in Britain than in West Germany. Furthermore the time required to produce one Escort is about 21 man-hours in West Germany and 40 man-hours in Britain. The West German plant turns out 1,200 cars a day with 7,762 workers, and the British plant produces 800 of the same cars a day with 10,040 workers.

Table 2

LABOR AND WAGE COSTS FOR AUTOMOBILE WORKERS IN FOUR AUTO-PRODUCING COUNTRIES (1981)

	Total Labor Costs Per Hour		Direct Hourly Wage		Direct Annual Wage	
	Local Currency	U.S. $ Equivalent*	Local Currency	U.S. $ Equivalent*	Local Currency	U.S. $ Equivalent*
Germany, West	DM 30.10	$13.55	DM 17.00	$ 7.65	DM 41,886 (Based on 13-month year and 43.9-hour week)	$18,848
Japan	Yen 2,736	$13.68	Yen 2,052	$10.26	Yen 4,481,156 (Including annual and semiannual bonuses, family allowances. Based on 42-hour week.)	$22,405
United Kingdom	£ 4.53	$ 8.70	£ 2.90	$ 5.57	£ 6,045 (Based on 40-hour week.)	$11,606
United States	$ 22.00		$ 11.76		$ 24,460 (Based on 39.9 hour-week.)	

*1982.
Sources: Eurostat, *Hourly Earnings, Hours of Work, 1980*; International Labor Office, *Yearbook of Labor Statistics, 1980*; and various publications of the OECD, interviews, articles, newspaper reports and general updates.

149

The Honda Ballade, made in Japan, and the Triumph Acclaim, produced in Britain, are identical machines in all respects except for certain additions to the Honda car that are needed to meet Japanese environmental standards. If anything, the Ballade is slightly more complex and expensive to make for that reason. Before Honda and BL Ltd. agreed to coproduce the cars in their respective countries, studies done by the two companies established some startling facts about productivity. The production of one car takes 13 hours of direct labor (all people who work directly on the assembly line to produce all phases of the car) in Japan and 20 hours in the United Kingdom. The British plant employs 20,000 workers to manufacture the same number of cars that are made by 13,000 workers in Japan.

The fact that Japanese workers are paid nearly twice as much as their British counterparts (see Table 2) is more than offset by the superior productivity of the Japanese work force. There are many reasons for this exceptional productivity and worker attitude is clearly one of the most important. However, this is not to say that Japanese workers are better than British workers but rather that they are more highly motivated and have better organization from top to bottom.

In Japan, supplies for assembly-line production wait only 48 hours in the warehouse before delivery and use at the plant. In Western Europe and the United States it can take weeks for supplies to be delivered and the materials can sit for weeks before being used. The number of support workers, the element of indirect labor that comprises maintenance, management and all those workers who do not actually participate in the manufacturing process, is much smaller in Japan than in the other major auto-producing nations.

Another advantage is the educational system in Japan, which turns out highly trained, engineering-oriented workers who can be taught the most sophisticated machinery faster than workers in Western Europe and the United States. Finally, the collectivist attitude, the loyalty of employers and employees to each other and to the firm and the executive selection process all enhance the efficiency and lower the costs of Japanese auto manufacturing.

Low labor costs and high productivity are key elements of success in today's automobile market. This will remain true until the day prohibitive trade barriers are erected or ownership of a car is no longer deemed an essential component of a decent standard of living. And that day is very likely not far off. Then the export-dependent Japanese economy will suffer. Until that time auto-producing countries with high labor costs and low productivity will continue to suffer economic disruptions. For the first time UAW is negotiating a contract that calls for a reduction in benefits and labor costs, which will effectively lower salaries. A slowing down of salary increases in both labor and management at BL Ltd. in the United Kingdom, Fiat in Italy and Volkswagen in West Germany is setting a precedent for all manufacturing industries. Workers are being laid off in these countries and plants are being shut down for lack of consumer demand. In the United States hundreds of thousands of auto workers are out of work, capital for reinvestment is nearly dried up and the future of the auto industry seems black.

In the United States the big automakers are attempting to reduce the size and salaries of their management staffs. Ford, for example, currently has a salaried management staff proportionally twice the size of Toyota's and has 12 layers of decision-making hierarchy compared to about seven at Toyota. Tentative and badly needed steps are being made to correct this situation. Even the excessively large salaries of top executives are being trimmed.

When the auto industry suffers, the entire economy built

upon it falters. Businesses dependent on the sale and maintenance of new cars and those dependent on travel by car as well as many other segments of the commercial network feel the pains of retraction. Tax revenues decline and the combined effects of this downturn can soon spread to the entire economy.

The airline industry is another transportation sector in serious difficulty, although its problems are not related to the manufacture of equipment. Only a few manufacturers have the resources to produce the huge, expensive jetliners required by all national airlines and they must keep their costs and output competitive at all times because of the huge investments involved. A heavily overpriced aircraft will soon fail in the marketplace.

Aircraft are designed with the exact needs of the customers in mind. Usually the equipment is pretested before it's bought and often preordered in sufficient quantities before it's manufactured to assure initial financial success. Fuel consumption of comparable aircraft is a critical competitive factor among airlines. In recent years airlines have preferred to modify older machines to use less fuel rather than to order new ones. This practice and a decline in passenger and cargo business have led to smaller orders for aircraft from the manufacturers, and the shrinkage of new orders is a painful symptom of a troubled industry in general.

The major problems of the airline industry stem from the fact that there are too many national carriers for the number of customers. Most of the airlines carry too much overhead, with too many people being paid too much for the amount of business being done. The international airlines lost between $2.6 billion and $3 billion in 1981, and there is every reason to believe that this situation will get worse unless there are major reforms in staffing levels and salaries and a general curtailment in flight operations.

The largest international airlines—Pan Am, TWA, British Airways, Lufthansa, Air France, Japan Air Lines, El Al, Alitalia, KLM, Swissair—have acknowledged financial difficulties and have been cutting back personnel and salaries in an effort to reduce overhead. The next table (3) lists total passenger/kilometers (the number of passengers multiplied by the number of kilometers flown), the number of pilots and copilots, the total number of employees and the number of passenger/kilometers per employee for 10 leading international carriers in 1980.

Many countries consider their airlines to be sources of national prestige; therefore profitability is not the decisive factor in their operation. These airlines, however, compete for international passengers, reducing the revenues of the profit-oriented carriers. Table 4 gives the same type of information as Table 3 for five carriers with an inefficiently high ratio of employees per passenger/kilometers.

The number of people employed by different airlines varies to a remarkable degree. Some payrolls are far greater than others, both because of the number of employees and the different ranges of pay for what are frequently identical or very similar jobs. For example, jet captains for American carriers earn between $80,000 and $110,000 a year on international routes; copilots earn from $45,000 to $66,000. On British Airways captains earn £22,261 ($42,964) and senior jet captains make £27,733 ($53,524) at the top of the scale. Copilots range from a beginning £12,613 ($24,343) to £19,106 ($36,875) at the top.

The pay of jet pilots and crews in the industrialized countries generally follows the earnings pattern of middle-level business executives, with Swiss, Belgian and West German pilots and crews leading the list. The perks for all pilots, including per diem expense allowances and time off, are important elements in the pay package and vary from airline

Table 3

STAFFING AND PERFORMANCE IN PASSENGER/KILOMETERS OF
10 INTERNATIONAL AIRLINES (1980)

	Passenger/Km (millions)	Number of Pilots & Copilots	Total Number of Employees	Passenter/Km Flown per Employee
British Airways	38,355	2,542	51,955	738,235
Japan Air Lines	21,339	1,172	21,242	1,004,566
Air France	21,258	1,313	33,215	640,012
Lufthansa	18,932	1,481	30,664	617,401
Trans World Airlines	15,940	2,142	33,145	475,758
Qantas Airways	15,769	545	13,702	1,150,853
KLM	14,058	748	18,968	171,142
Alitalia	11,194	1,198	18,243	613,605
Air Canada	11,096	1,902	23,139	479,536
Swissair	10,618	905	15,356	691,456

Table 4

FIVE INTERNATIONAL AIRLINES WITH LARGER THAN AVERAGE STAFFS PER PASSENGER/KILOMETERS

	Passenger/Km (millions)	Number of Pilots & Copilots	Total Number of Employees	Passenger/Km Flown per Employee
Pakistan International	4,522	400	23,581	191,764
Iraqi Airways	1,083	124	5,316	203,724
Egypt Air	2,536	219	9,682	261,929
Saudia	4,958	541	18,775	264,074
Aeromexico	2,908	705	8,363	347,722

Source: IATA, *World Air Transport Statistics 1980;* and private analysis.

155

to airline. The pay scales for flight attendants of Western and Japanese airlines are similar, averaging from $12,000 to $21,000 with time and grade.

The lower end of the scale is exemplified by the income of senior Indian jet captains, 164,700 rupees ($18,300) a year. However, this salary combined with the perks that go with the job make Indian pilots the highest salaried employee category in the country. Moreover the prestige of the job is enormous; Prime Minister Indira Gandhi's older son was a jet captain for many years, further enhancing the prestige of an already highly desirable job. Also in the lower pay range are pilots for South Africa Airline, who make 18,240 rand ($19,200) a year.

The airline industry is a unique example of overstaffing at many levels and frequent overpayment of personnel that has caused near disaster for several of the large national carriers. At the same time, smaller airlines have managed to continue with subsidies that minimize the losses caused by economic inefficiency. Nevertheless several of these as well as many large airlines are trimming their budgets, including salaries, and curtailing flight activities in keeping with the general economic downturn affecting the world's transportation industries.

Another crucial, if less glamorous, means of transportation is shipping, both of cargo and people. Many developed countries have merchant marines that are closely regulated by union agreements and national and international laws of vessel safety and registration. In other countries, such as Liberia and Greece, regulations governing shipping are much more lax. On ships registered by most Western countries salaries range from about $40,000 to $55,000 for captains of large vessels, including large oil tankers. There is also a very generous vacation schedule, amounting in some cases to 130 days a year. The average wage for officers below captain on such ships is about $550 a week, but again the range varies considerably from country to country.

An ordinary seaman on a ship registered in the United States earned $675 a month base pay in 1980, and with overtime he could easily have made over $12,000 a year. In addition he was entitled to approximately 10 days off for every month worked and food and berth provided on the job. Those with higher ratings, such as electricians, can earn over $18,000 a year with overtime plus vacation and benefits. Wage scales are roughly equivalent in other Western countries except for the United Kingdom, where they are lower, and West Germany, Sweden, Belgium and the Netherlands, where they tend to be higher.

The jobs and the incomes they provide in the transportation industries are numerous and their range is complex. Some flourish while others decline; the troubles of the airline and automobile industries have increased the use of mass transportation—bus, subway, train, and even boat. In many countries the infrastructure of mass travel is in desperate need of modernization; in some countries it has yet to be built.

11

CRIME

In the spring of 1981 federal authorities in the United States noted a marked increase in the number of deaths caused by overdoses of heroin. In the first three weeks of May 1981 alone, there were 14 reported deaths from this cause, and the annual rate was running considerably higher than the average for previous years. The reason, it was determined, was mainly due to an increased availability of the undiluted drug through illegal channels from the Middle East and Asia. This, in turn, increased the strength of heroin sold on the street from the normal 3% pure to a new high of 7%, creating a more powerful and deadly dosage for about the same price.

The international drug trade has become a $150 billion business with profits ranging from $45 billion to $70 billion a year. 1981 was a bumper crop year for opium poppies grown in Thailand, Laos, Burma and Pakistan, and an estimated 500 to 600 tons of heroin were grown around the world, much of it destined for the United States. The markup from producer to distributor to street salesmen is at least 15 to 20 times the original purchase price of heroin, and the sums that can be earned in this deadly trade are matched only by the risks involved to the shipper, the distributor and the pusher from law enforcement authorities and, even more importantly, from other drug traffickers.

In some countries the export of drugs has become a major factor in the economy. The export of cocaine from Bolivia is a business so large and lucrative that the government is deeply dependent on it. Official connivance and cooperation, not to mention investment, in the Bolivian drug trade by high officials has caused the downfall of several governments. The International Monetary Fund and the United States government have stipulated that the current government of General Celso Villa must make some effort to control this trade as a prerequisite for continued cooperation and aid.

Hashish is known as "the oil of Lebanon" and it is estimated that over 2,000 tons are grown annually in the Bekaa Valley, earning about $500 million in the international drug market. In fact in Baalbek and other cities of the region the money from this trade is openly used to build roads, factories, homes and schools. The growing and sale of hashish has become a central support of the economy.

Even more striking is the economic role of the trade in marijuana and cocaine from Colombia to the United States and the rest of the world. Until a few years ago Colombian coffee, with annual sales of about $1.5 billion a year, was the nation's largest export commodity. Now the sale of marijuana and cocaine produced in Colombia and smuggled into the southern United States through Mexico, Jamaica, the Bahamas and other islands accounts for almost $5 billion a year. Colombia has become another country that relies upon a drug-exporting economy, and a new class of drug millionaires, with heavily guarded estates, bands of retainers and all manner of luxuries that stagger the imagination has emerged.

Southern Florida, particularly Miami, has become a center of the international drug traffic. Much of the enormous real estate boom and increase in investments of all kinds in the area stems from the massive influx of drug-earned capital. The underground economy in southern Florida is estimated at almost $40 billion a year, a major proportion of which comes from the drug trade. Law enforcement officials claim that in 1981 from $7 billion to $10 billion was made by drug smugglers in the area, who provided 70% of all marijuana and cocaine consumed in the United States and a large proportion of the drugs that reached Europe.

An essential part of the underground economy in Miami and one related mainly, though not entirely, to drugs is the laundering of money. So blatant is this changing of traceable, illegal money into clean currency that the Federal Reserve Bank in Miami is the only branch of the American Reserve System that regularly reports a cash surplus. Cash is literally carried into local banks in suitcases and shoe boxes and deposited for transfer into other bills or invested in municipal bonds and other forms of tax-exempt holdings with few reporting requirements. Through this laundering the original cash is quickly disposed of. It is not surprising that in this part of Florida, as in all places around the world where drugs are a major source of income—Colombia, Bolivia, Turkey, Pakistan, Laos, processing centers in Europe—violent crime is very much a part of daily life.

The incomes of individuals trafficking in drugs are of course extremely hard to uncover; one of the requirements for success in this illegal trade is the ability to hide the financial details of the business. However, when a major ring is broken up, figures given out by the authorities offer some indication of the potential earnings involved.

In June 1981 a prominent Florida attorney, a marina owner and 10 other people were indicted for allegedly directing a marijuana-smuggling ring operating between Key West, Florida and Colombia. Officials estimated that the group made over $300 million from 1977 to 1980, making it one of the largest illegal drug operations ever uncovered in the United States to date. That same month French police raided a heroin laboratory in Marseille, France and seized 34 pounds of a morphine-base drug being prepared there, which they claimed was worth $2 million. In August $48 million worth of cocaine was seized in an apartment in Van Nuys, California. These three cases—one huge, one medium and one small by drug trade standards—in the summer of 1981 illustrate the continual activity and internationality of the drug trade as well as the vast sums of money to be made. Every day some arrest is made in connection with smuggling.

In September 1981 four people were seized in New York City with handbags consigned to a fashion shop there. Hidden in the handbags were about 1,500 pounds of Lebanese hashish, worth well over $1 million in street value. Assuredly on the same day, as on any given day, all over the world transactions were being completed for millions of dollars worth of hashish, cocaine, marijuana and other drugs, and most escape the attention of the authorities. This international drug trade involves an intricate and interconnected network of growing, preparing, shipping, buying and selling that constitutes one of the world's principal commercial enterprises.

The illegal money made, from the billions at the organized network level down to the $150,000 that the pusher can easily earn in a year, depends largely on the demand of the addict. To satisfy a serious heroin habit requires about $30,000 a year, and there are perhaps 175,000 such addicts in the United States alone and at least another 50,000 in the other developed countries of the world. Therefore the total retail value of illegal drug purchases by addicts can be crudely estimated at $6.75 billion—or 15% more than the 1981 budget of Canada. Besides serious addicts there are millions of casual users who consume, on a worldwide basis, vast quantities of drugs. There are always customers eager to buy all types of drugs.

While less dangerous than the drug trade, white-collar crime is just as lucrative and complex; some experts think that the big illegal profits of the future are not in cocaine or heroin dealing but in computer embezzlement, stock frauds, municipal bond swindles, illegal tax shelters and inventive methods of laundering ill-gotten cash into legitimate investment capital. The Joint Economic Committee of the U.S. Congress estimated that such crime for personal and company gain cost about $45 billion in 1980-81 in the United States alone, and the worldwide figure may be another $40 billion. So extensive is white-collar crime that in recent years 233 of the famed Fortune 500 corporations have had criminal suits filed against them or some of their employees.

A recent symposium on international computer security brought attention to what may be the most potent white-collar crime of the next decade. Soon, according to computer experts, a corporation in one country will be able to ruin its competitors in another, and some day whole nations could be brought to their knees by theft of computer components and data. In 1981 a chemical company in West Germany paid a ransom of 450,000 marks ($202,500) for the return of 22 magnetic heads without which the firm literally could not function. This crime is a harbinger of threats that companies and nations will receive, and raises the problem of how to guard indispensable computer parts, equipment and data from thieves who are highly trained and know exactly what to steal. Theft of the right computer part is estimated, according to data on such crimes to date, to yield an average of $50,000, compared with about $10,000 for traditional industrial thefts, such as robbery, hijacking or diversion of produced items for illegal sale.

Several cases of illegal transfers of funds from one bank to another, often in a different country, by computer experts working for the banks have yielded millions of dollars. Wells Fargo was bilked out of $21 million by a flashy sports promoter who worked with an inside accomplice to foil the company's computer system. Chase Manhattan Bank was the victim of a less publicized case in which a vice president of the bank with 25 years of service used his authority to transfer electronically numerous loans of up to $3 million to borrowers who gave him kickbacks in a variety of deals. His personal gains before he was caught have never been officially stated, but on a total electronic diversion of $20 million they amounted to several million dollars.

A pervasive and major form of white-collar crime involving businesses in their dealings with foreign companies and governments is bribery of officials and others in positions of power to obtain favorable contracts or simply to beat out competing firms for the same job. Certain countries are notorious for the corrupt practices surrounding business dealings; in Saudi Arabia it is impossible to negotiate for any large business investment without the intercession of a member of the Saudi royal family: a prince, of whom there are 5,000 in the country. Some princes expect a bribe of $10,000 to $100,000 for their help in making a deal; others with greater influence expect and receive a great deal more. In 1980 one key government minister is reported to have received $500 million in "commission fees" for working with companies from West Germany, Japan, the United Kingdom, France and the United States.

Indonesia and Malaysia are two of the principal countries in Asia where bribes are essential for the successful completion of business arrangements. In Argentina and Mexico there is an average markup of between 15% and 20% on the value of contracts, and many countries look upon bribes simply as necessary business expenses. The biggest bribe payers for closing of deals and obtaining favorable contracts in competitive situations are France, West Germany, Japan, Korea and Switzerland, but no industrialized nation is far behind.

Bribes range in size from the $10 to $500 paid to minor officials to grease the bureaucratic wheels to the millions of dollars often doled out to assure success in a major negotiation. The latter are given official sanction in many countries of Africa, such as Kenya and Nigeria, and in the Persian Gulf, where national laws require that a local citizen or company own at least half of any foreign firm established there.

In Nigeria native entrepreneurs offer their expertise in charting a foreign investment through the layers of bureaucracy and various bribery requirements. In this system bribes are piled on top of one another, almost like a value-added tax. If a deal involves a $100 million investment, a French or Japanese or German firm will plan on an additional $10 million or so for the services of their native partners and more in smaller sums to hasten the negotiation down the line. These entrepreneurs are richly rewarded, as high as 20% or more of the value of a total contract.

Investors from industrialized countries learn the national characteristics of their partners and what little touches can make bribery more attractive within the local cultural context. For example, some Asians are renowned for their love of gambling, and one fine way to pass on money is to play incompetent golf with an important official and bet heavily on the game. Should the day of the negotiation be impossibly crowded with meetings, an after-dinner poker game with the key officials is arranged, the prospective investor being sure that he loses the requisite amount before the evening is over.

In Mexico and Argentina negotiations for contracts frequently take place with female company present. This is very popular in Mexico, where $120-a-night call girls are used to set the proper mood for business discussions. In Argentina gifts of jewelry and objets d'art are always welcome.

Kidnapping is a crime that has frequently taken on an international context, and has many faces. Political kidnapping, for example, the Red Brigade's abduction of General James Dozier, is not done for financial gain. In recent years there have been many such kidnappings, not to mention assassinations, for political causes.

Another kind of kidnapping is committed solely for monetary gain, even if relatively small. For example, the abduction of six-year-old Oron Yarden in Israel for $43,000 ransom, which was paid, is just one of hundreds of kidnappings for money that occur around the world almost daily. The ransoms can go from a few thousand dollars for one life to as much as the traffic will bear, as in the case of Chinese restaurant owner Tsung Ting Wang, who in 1981 was seized in New York on one day and returned the next for the sum of $100,000.

The number of attacks on international businessmen, who have the financial support of their companies and whose very presence in a country can be exploited as a political pretext for terrorist kidnappings, has grown in the past decade. Terrorist attacks on foreign businessmen occur about eight times daily around the world, and an estimated $150 million in ransom has been paid out by businesses. Out of 567 kidnappings recorded by Business International in the years 1970 to 1980, 35 resulted in the death of the victim.

One of the highest ransoms ever paid was the $14.3 million given to Argentine terrorists in 1973 by Exxon to free employee Victor Samuelson. Ironically his relatives and shareholders of Exxon later brought a class-action suit against the company for return of the money, claiming executives exceeded their authority in paying the ransom. In Italy there have been many cases of terrorists abducting well-known businessmen, who are favorite targets because of their obvious solvency. One such victim was industrialist Alberto Massoni of Milan, who was seized for a ransom of more than 7.2 billion lire ($5.7 million) in 1980. Massoni eventually escaped his captors, and a number of people have since been jailed for the crime.

The long list of kidnappings of international businessmen causes considerable consternation in the boardrooms of West German, French, American, British and Japanese multinational corporations. Needless to say, the kidnapping/ransom insurance business has grown by leaps and bounds to keep pace with the incidence of the crime. Annual premiums now amount to about $80 million, and approximately 25% of multinationals carry such insurance; expectations are that this figure will reach 50% within five years. Not only is the kidnapping of businessmen, when successful, very lucrative but it also increases the costs of investing companies along with the unavoidable bribery payments.

A type of white-collar crime that has become more common recently is smuggling cash from one country to another to avoid taxation or seizure of excessive or illegal profits or simply the holdings of wealthy people. The traffic in smuggled cash between France and Switzerland, for example, has increased since the Socialist government of Francois Mitterand came to power. Wealthy Frenchmen, fearful of having their wealth seized, employ detectives to carry funds across the border for placement in secret-numbered Swiss accounts. Vast sums of money, whole family fortunes, have been transferred out of France in this manner. More sophisticated methods of smuggling funds are also employed, including electronic bank transfers and double-billing techniques. However, most of the money still goes by hand, and the fee for such service runs from 4% to 7% of the total value of the smuggled money. To make it worthwhile, smugglers require a minimum value for a transfer of 20 million francs to 30 million francs ($3.6 million to $5.4 million).

Crime characteristics vary remarkably from country to country around the world. One form of illegal activity that appears to flourish wherever there is taxation, which is to say nearly everywhere, is the underground economy, or the movement of "black money." In a strictly national context this can be in the form of undeclared profits, hidden business activities or bribes for consumer services and business arrangements (not to be confused with foreign bribes discussed earlier).

In China the *People's Daily* frequently denounces bribe paying in the form of better food, more comfortable housing or travel abroad to assure the cooperation of officials, or simply a cigarette to the butcher for better meat. One curiously common category of articles traded on the Chinese black market is equipment illegally salvaged from closed-down or abandoned factories. Such tools and materials are sought for use either in illegal private enterprises or to improve the efficiency of legitimate plants in need of repair and thereby win acclaim for the bureaucrat in charge.

The population of Prato, Italy enjoys a median income that is about 50% higher than the national average. They work in local industries that manufacture textile fashions, some of which are sold to Italy's world-famous design houses. These small-scale businesses do not declare all their profits or sales on their tax statements. Similar complexes of cottage industries manufacturing textiles and leather products, including handbags, shoes etc., abound throughout the country and constitute an underground economy. Although this *economia sommersa* does not pay anywhere near its full share of taxes, if any at all, it is one of the most productive aspects of the Italian economy and accounts for as much as 30% or more of the national product than the official figures report. It is made possible by hidden employment, second and undeclared jobs.

Whether destroying this illegal economy with all its untaxed money would be to the national advantage is a real question. Such economies exist throughout Europe and reflect the resistance of citizens to taxation and, in many instances, to planned economies.

In countries of the European Community and others that have a value-added tax, those who run the black economy must be very devious to avoid detection by the authorities. In the United Kingdom a man may hire a builder for £380 ($730) to alter his living room. The builder gets the materials and pays the tax on them, passing the cost along to his employer. At the same time, by mutual agreement, he has ordered enough materials to refurbish a fireplace in the same room, for perhaps another £150 ($290). He declares the initial job on his income tax but not the refurbishment of the fireplace. He is thus able to save money on his taxes and pass along some of the savings to his employer in the form of lower cost for the fireplace job. This is a very common practice in many industrialized countries, such as the United Kingdom, France, Belgium and especially Scandinavian countries, and the amount of income produced is estimated to range from 15% to 30% of the total economy.

The underground economy flourishes in the Communist

nations of Eastern Europe and even in the Soviet Union, according to numerous reports by emigrants from that country. Bids for top government jobs in the Azerbaidzhan region over the past 10 years supposedly ranged from 100,000 rubles to 250,000 rubles ($74,000 to $185,000), depending upon how much the holders of these jobs could expect in future bribes.

Illegally made items, called ''left hand'' goods, are produced in the major urban centers, such as Moscow, Odessa, Riga, Tiflis and elsewhere. Tens of thousands of these left-hand factories, according to reports, manufacture knitwear, shoes, sunglasses, recordings of Western music, handbags and other consumer items demanded by citizens who have very little to spend their incomes on except food and drink. The successful underground entrepreneurs, however, have great difficulty enjoying their wealth because the least sign of sudden or ostentatious spending in a closed society brings the authorities running.

An underground jewelry merchant in Moscow was illegally earning about 450,000 rubles ($333,000) a year. Since he could not spend it on the yachts, cars, dachas or vacations earmarked for government officials and certain artists, professors and others, he was reduced to cramming his little apartment with boxes of rubles. Soon the jeweler's cache was discovered; before he was to be tried, he died of cancer. He was literally a victim of an embarrassment of riches, a situation not so uncommon in Communist societies, where most payments are in benefits and there is little to spend illegal cash on without grave risk.

In most countries of the world violent crime becomes a more serious problem every year. Much of this increase has been attributed to the accessibility of cheap handguns, particularly in the United States. There were about 340,000 violent crimes involving handguns in the United

States in 1980 compared with 171 such crimes involving handguns in Japan in 1979 and 300 in West Germany the same year.

According to the FBI, the number of armed robberies, bank robberies, burglaries and larcenies in the first six months of 1980 totaled 3,459, and the value of the stolen money and property amounted to $22.1 million, or about $6,389 per crime. The FBI also investigated 5,174 bank fraud and embezzlement cases during the same period, a substantial increase over the same six months of the previous year.

These figures greatly surpass those for most other industrialized countries, although the number of crimes and the amount of money illegally taken through bank fraud and embezzlement is the same almost everywhere except in Japan and some other highly tradition-oriented societies of Asia. The crime rate in Japan is one of the lowest in the world, and the police there are recognized to be among the most effective and disciplined anywhere.

Italy suffers from endless violent kidnappings and other terrorist crimes. West Germany, France, Belgium and the Scandinavian countries have flourishing black economies aimed at avoiding extensive taxes. The United Kingdom has a hidden working class with undeclared incomes and a white-collar crime rate that grows with the stagnation of the economy. The United States is plagued by drug traffic and violent crime, and new forms of white-collar fraud and embezzlement are invented daily as the economy becomes ever more complex.

Bribery and corruption have become more prevalent than ever in the developing countries, where foreign investment and multinational industries present increasing opportunities for the sale of favors and quick illegal profits. Violent crime is also becoming a more serious problem in African countries, such as Kenya and Nigeria, in Central America and in parts of Asia, where in recent years piracy on the high seas has become a common practice. The list of criminal activities and the money to be made from them demonstrates that crime is, unfortunately, one of the world's great growth industries.

INDEX